OFFICIAL HISTORY

OF THE

BAY OF PIGS OPERATION

VOLUME II

PARTICIPATION IN THE CONDUCT

OF FOREIGN POLICY

(pages 1-167)

Published by Books Express Publishing
Copyright © Books Express, 2011
ISBN 978-1-780394-74-9

Books Express publications are available from all good retail and online booksellers. For
publishing proposals and direct ordering please contact us at: info@books-express.com

CENTRAL INTELLIGENCE AGENCY

OFFICIAL HISTORY
OF THE
BAY OF PIGS OPERATION

Volume II

PARTICIPATION IN THE CONDUCT

OF FOREIGN POLICY

October 1979

Jack B. Pfeiffer

FOREWORD

Nearly 20 years have elapsed since the Agency
was authorized by President Eisenhower to undertake
a program of covert action to overthrow Fidel Castro,
but despite voluminous writings subsequent to the
activity intending to show the disastrous nature of
CIA's guidance of the operation, no attention ever
has focused on the Agency's participatory role in
the formulation of United States foreign policy vis-
a-vis Guatemala and Nicaragua during the course of
the operation. One purpose of this volume in the
Official History of the Bay of Pigs series is to
examine in detail the extent of those relationships
as they impacted on -- or in fact became -- the
policies of the United States government toward those
two countries.

In Guatemala, the Agency dealt directly with
the President Miguel Ydigoras Fuentes or his personal
representative Roberto Alejos; and the relationships
were far more complex -- and covered a longer time
span -- than was the case with Nicaragua. In addition,

negotiations initiated by the Agency with the Government of Guatemala heavily involved both the Departments of State and Defense; and, during the Eisenhower administration, the Special Group.

The Nicaraguan story principally concerned the Agency's efforts to obtain an air base and port facility for launching the anti-Castro strike force against Cuba; and the involvement was directly with the President of Nicaragua, Luis Somoza Debayle, and his brother, Anastasio Somoza Debayle, the Commander of Nicaragua's Armed Forces. The US embassy in Nicaragua and its representatives were kept informed and, in general, supported the Agency as the ball carrier with the Government of Nicaragua. The story was relatively straightforward with the Agency being given the green light to negotiate in many areas affecting US relations with that country.

A third Central American country, Panama, was involved marginally in the Agency's anti-Castro effort. Forts Randolph and Sherman in the Canal Zone were the sites initially selected for PM and communications training for the cadres which were to help organize the dissident elements inside Cuba; and France airfield in the Zone also was used by Agency aircraft during the course of the project. CIA's negotiations for use of these Panama sites, therefore, were with the US Departments of Defense and Army, rather than with the government of Panama.

As the anti-Castro program of the US was implemented, a sometimes embarrassing relationship with the United Kingdom developed because of the frequency with which aircraft of the anti-Castro Brigade made emergency landings on the airstrip at Grand Caymen Island and, in one instance, at Kingston, Jamaica. Agency personnel assigned to the anti-Castro project were not directly involved in the negotiations with the senior UK representatives for release of either the aircraft or their crews. Acting upon instructions received from the DCI level, CIA's [redacted] [redacted] was principally responsible for resolving such problems; and, consequently, such negotiations are not subject to discussion in this volume.[*]

---

* The topic is discussed in Volume I of this history, *Air Operations*.

As with the preceding volume of this series,
the author wishes to acknowledge the contributions
of the other members of the CIA History Staff, Mrs.
Sharon Bond and Mrs. Eulalie Hammond, to the completion of this segment of the Bay of Pigs history.
From substantive research to typing and proofreading,
they did whatever needed doing regardless of their
job descriptions. For any errors of fact or questions
of interpretation, they are blameless -- the author
assumes full responsibility.

VOLUME II

Contents

The clearest case to me of the CIA
affecting directly negotiations with
another Chief of State was Ydigoras.
I think that was frankly unavoidable
and inescapable, because we had almost
constant problems of a kind of operational nature. Here we were training
a force that [Col.] Jack Hawkins once
characterized to me as the most powerful
military force from Mexico to Colombia
in his [Ydigoras's] country. He himself
faced a lot of domestic opposition --
at one time they tried to overthrow him,
as you remember. He wanted to get this
[Cuban] group out of there as soon as
possible, and I am sure that you have
seen a lot of the traffic and memoranda
of discussion; but it seems to me really
to characterize especially the period in
November-December (1960) when Tom Mann
wanted to get the Brigade the hell out
of Guatemala and Ydigoras would have
welcomed it. There was no place for
them to go. I still remember that we
even talked about ferrying them to that
training site _____ in
_____, which was a measure of the des-
peration -- or desperate desire -- to
get them out of there [Guatemala]. We
talked again about trying to find a remote
site in the continental US, but Tom Mann
with the State Department would have none
of that. In that period when sort of
constant operational problems with Ydigoras
were all wrapped up in the larger question
of where this training activity could be
carried on and how it could be made less
obtrusive -- I think it was just inevi-
table that Agency representatives found
themselves dealing directly with Ydigoras.

Richard M. Bissell
to Jack B. Pfeiffer
17 October 1975

THE BAY OF PIGS OPERATION

Volume II Participation in the Conduct
of Foreign Policy

Part I
Guatemala

A. Background

Direct participation in the affairs of Guatemala
was not new in Agency history. In 1954 CIA had provided support and had motivated Guatemalan forces which
ousted then President Castillo Armas, a pro-communist,
in favor of the presidency of Jacobo Arbenz Guzmann.

On 26 July 1957 Arbenz was assassinated and the
political situation in Guatemala evolved into a three-
way dog fight among the forces of the left, the right,
and the center.

and were

opposed to both the leftists and to the party of
Ydigoras Fuentes -- the rightist candidate who also
had the support of the Army. When it became clear

that Ydigoras was

the most popular figure in Guatemala

[   ] .. arranging
for a behind the scenes conference between
Ydigoras and the MDN [Cruz Salazar's party].
A "deal" was arranged whereby the assembly
would elect Ydigoras and the MDN would get
three seats in the cabinet, forgiveness
for the sins committed under the Castillo
regime, and a financial "pay-off" to Cruz
and other MDN leaders. On 12 February 1958
the Assembly elected Ydigoras as President. 1/

In the interval from the election of Ydigoras

until the announcement of Eisenhower's anti-Castro

program, both the government of Guatemala and, through

the Agency, the United States Government began to

focus closer attention on Fidel Castro's revolution

which led to the overthrow of the Batista government

at the beginning of 1959. Although the Department of

State hesitated to classify Castro as a communist,

there was little doubt among Clandestine Services

personnel about the direction in which Castro was

tending; and by the early part of 1960, it was clear

that the Government of Guatemala (GOG) was willing to

take some risks in opposition to Fidel Castro. Not

only did Guatemala sever official relations with Cuba,

but before the end of February 1960, President Ydigoras

offered the use of his territory to support propaganda

activities directed against Castro; and he also made

a specific offer through the CIA "to groups favorably regarded by us [of] training facilities in the Petén area of Guatemala." 2/*

B. Establishing Contacts with Ydigoras and Alejos

It was more than two months following President Eisenhower's announcement of an anti-Castro program before Chief JMATE, Jacob D. Esterline, and [ ]

[ ] Robert K. Davis, met with representatives of the GOG; but in the interval between the announcement and Esterline's first meeting, Davis had already established contact with Roberto Alejos -- the principal representative of President Ydigoras Fuentes in all

---

* It is interesing to observe that this specific reference to the use of the Petén area in Guatemala was reworded for use by the DCI in a memorandum to the members of the Special Group to read "this training and holding [of anti-Castro Cubans] would be conducted in a secure remote area of a friendly Latin American country." 3/ The Special Group 5412 was a group composed of the Assistant Secretaries of State and Defense, the DCI, the President's National Security Adviser, and a CIA Secretariat. Its principal purpose was to review proposed paramilitary and clandestine operations and to provide guidance on such proposals for the President. President Eisenhower made extensive use of this group, but President Kennedy largely abandoned it until late in the period of the Bay of Pigs operation.

subsequent matters involving the CIA.* Esterline incidentally, had been the senior officer in the Headquarters end of the operation which had forced the
resignation and ouster of President Arbenz in 1954.
During the first meetings with Alejos and Ydigoras
in Guatemala City on 30 and 31 May 1960, plans were
initiated for the use of a portion of Alejos's coffee
plantation -- Finca Helvetia -- as a communications
training site; and discussions were held concerning
additional sites for the training of paramilitary
candidates.

At the same time, it was made clear to Ydigoras
that the Agency sponsored Cuban exile organization,
the Frente Revolucionario Democrático (FRD), would
nominally be responsible for whatever training activities of Cubans took place in Guatemala. The names
of Antonio Varona and Justo Carrillo were given to
President Ydigoras and Robert Alejos as two of the

---

* Eisenhower's anti-Castro program was dated 17 March
1960. CIA's anti-Castro effort was located within the
Western Hemisphere Division, Branch 4 (WH/4). Initially
WH/4 was given the crypt JMARC; but when this was com-
promised, the crypt was changed to JMATE. Throughout
this history, except when direct quotations are given,
the term JMATE is used.

key figures in the FRD. According to Esterline's report of the meeting "it was never said in so many words that CIA, in effect, is supporting these people, it was implicit in President Ydigoras's attitude that he well understood that support is being given to these people through indirect means."* In playing his own game of plausible deniability, Ydigoras pointed out that the less he knew of the operation, the better would be his denials to the Organization of American States (OAS) or others who were concerned that anti-Castro activities were being mounted within his country's borders. It was also during this first session between Chief, WH/4 and the Guatemalans that plans were made to introduce Esterline to the Guatemalan ambassador

---

* Arthur Schlesinger put the situation quite accurately in the following comment:

> The Frente was appropriately named: it was a front and nothing more. While its members talked among themselves, CIA was engaged in a recruiting drive among Cuban refugees in Florida and Central America. It had also persuaded President Ydigoras of Guatemala to permit the establishment of a secret training camp and air base in the Guatemalan mountains." 3a/

in Washington, Carlos Alejos, the brother of Roberto Alejos. 4/*

Portents of things to come followed shortly after Esterline's first meeting with Roberto Alejos. On 8 June 1960, Alejos, as he had indicated in his initial meeting with Davis and Esterline, was in the United States where he met with Esterline. Among the subjects discussed, in addition to the utilization of Guatemalan territory for the training of anti-Castro Cubans, Alejos said that he would be taking a look at the airstrip at Retalhuleu to see if it was capable of handling C-54 aircraft. Construction and renovation of this airstrip would later give rise to both some intra-agency squabbles and also some strain in the relationships between the Agency and Alejos.

At this time, too, Alejos was very much concerned about the United States ambassador to the OAS, John Dryer, who, according to Alejos, was pressing the GOG

---

* Carlos Alejos apparently was appointed US ambassador a short time prior to Esterline's meeting with Ydigoras and Roberto Alejos. A cable to the Department from Guatemala City on 18 May 1960 noted that Carlos Alejos "Ambassador-designate to the US" would arrive in New Orleans on 25 May 60. 4a/

to respond to a Cuban charge that Guatemala was being
used as a staging base for a planned invasion of Cuba
and that an OAS inspection was in order. Alejos's
response was that if Cuba would agree to a similar
inspection, Guatemala could be freely visted by the
OAS team. In what would be a continuing irritant
through the course of Project JMATE, Roberto Alejos
also expressed his displeasure with the failures of
the governments of Honduras and El Salvador to break
relations with Fidel Castro's Cuba. 5/

Whether Esterline actually met with Ambassador
Carlos Alejos at this time is not known, but it appears
possible that such a meeting may have taken place.*
In any event a cable sent from Guatemala City to the
Guatemalan Embassy in Washington, D. C. for Roberto
Alejos dated 7 June 1960, addressed itself in part
to Raul Roa's (Cuba's Foreign Minister) request for

---

* One of Roberto Alejos's cards with the following
note (translated from Spanish) was found in Chief,
WH/4 records:

. Carolio:
    The bearer is a good friend, I pray
    that you will assist him and make use of
    his contacts in the US.

the OAS investigation of Guatemala, and it also contains the following tantalizing message:

> Impossible to give proof of what is
> happening in Cuba[.] Members of the
> Premier's personal guard have been shot
> [according to] some sources of informa-
> tion. 6/*

By mid-June 1960 plans were well in hand for
establishing training activities in Guatemala. Roberto
Alejos, who had gone from Washington to Miami, had
been introduced to Casimiro (Chick) Barquin of DPD --
the Agency's air arm -- who was about to take off for
Guatemala to survey the airfields at San Jose and Retalhuleu, to check the airstrip at Petén, and to see what
other airstrips might be available. Robert Davis,

was in Miami to perform the introductions.
As proved to be the case in Nicragua,

Guatemala planned to isolate   activities
from the PM and communications training programs which

---

* In Spanish the message read as follows:

> PRUEBAS LO QUE PASA EN CUBA IMPOSIBLE DARLAS
> FUSILARIAN MIEMBROS GUARDIA PERSONAL PREMIER
> UNA DE LAS TANTAS FUENTES INFORMATION STOP.

Apparently in the transmission or in the cablese
some words and punctuation were lost, omitted, or
goofed up.

were about to be established. But unlike the Nicaraguan situation where ☐ was better able to do this, such isolation was more theoretical than practical. 7/

Davis did tell Roberto Alejos that matters pertaining to the training sites for the anti-Castro Cubans would henceforth be discussed with Juan Paula Argeo. Paula was a member of the FRD and it had been agreed between the head of the WH/4 political section, Gerald (Gerry) Droller, and the FRD that Paula would work out details of reimbursing Alejos during the course of this initial survey trip.* The funds were ostensibly coming from the FRD through Paula. In the course of arriving at decisions on the financing and the funding of the training, it was pointed out that Droller should urge the FRD leadership to increase its own fund raising program. 8/

While on the one hand the Agency was concerned with masking the funding for the FRD from the Cubans, it was at the same time concerned with disguising

---

* Droller was known to the Cubans as Frank Bender -- a cover identity that wasn't blown until the publication of Arthur Schlesinger's *A Thousand Days* in 1964. Juan Paula was, in fact, Manuel F. Goudie.

Alejos's position from the Cubans -- his role would be as a private Guatemalan citizen, cooperating with the FRD element for idealogical reasons. 9/ In addition to the Agency's interest in protecting the cover stories, Ydigoras himself was very much concerned that the training program not be revealed to the public. In one instance when he heard that a Guatemalan Congressman was trying to promote support for a group of pro-Batista Cuban recruits to overthrow Castro, he made it quite clear that such a program would find no support at the presidential level. Ydigoras even went so far as to suggest that perhaps he should expel a few pro-Batista and a few pro-Castro Cubans from Guatemala for propaganda purposes in order to protect the Agency's on-going operations. 10/*

By mid-July 1960, construction work had begun on the communications training base and the search was underway for a suitable airstrip. By early August, despite some reservations of the DPD element in charge

---

* Source reference numbers 11 and 12 not used.

- 10 -

of the air operations, it had been decided, particularly since it had been favored by the President of Guatemala, that the Retalhuleu airstrip, a graded sod-strip of approximately 4,300' in length, lying in the NW corner of Guatemala, roughly 40 km from the Pacific coast and 50 km from the Mexican border, would be expanded to 5,000'x100' with a crushed stone and asphalt surface. Suitable hanger type structures and other necessary airfield facilities would be installed at that site for the air training base. 13/

Although the details are given in another history, a word should be said here about the highly commendable performance of one of the Agency's engineers from the Office of Logistics, _____, who on 3 August 1960 was assigned to the Retalhuleu project as the resident engineer and who on 13 September saw President Ydigoras officially inaugurate the opening of the airstrip with the landing of some DC-3's, a C-46, and a couple of Aero Commanders. By 30 September all construction was completed including the extension of the airstrip to 5,000' and the base was ready for the inauguration of training activities. 14/*

---

* Despite some severe criticism from the A/DDP/A, C. Tracy Barnes, about cost overruns, inefficient
(footnote continued on following page)

C. Cover, Security and Latin Pride

A high degree of cooperation between the President of Guatemala and the Agency was clearly evident in the plans to provide a cover story for the increase of air activity at Retalhuleu. At the dedication of the base (JMADD), Ydigoras pointed out that the airfield was being renovated to provide protection for the northwest border of Guatemala and to provide a training base for new B-26's which were being acquired under the Military Assistance agreement with the United States. The infantry base (JMTRAV) was to be provided cover by GOG troops -- reportedly the palace guard for President Ydigoras -- who had begun training in the area in order to disguise Agency activities with the Cuban exiles.

In quest of support for his anti-Castro effort, Ydigoras was not reluctant to devise cover stories of his own. In the early part of August, for example, Ydigoras told Carl Jenkins, then COB JMTRAV, that he, Ydigoras, had "invented" a Cuban warship that was supposed to be lurking off of the east coast threatening

---

management by [   ], and similar other charges drawn exclusively from hindsight, rather than on-site investigation, Mr. [   ] did a magnificent job when faced with heavy obstacles, not the least of which was approximately 100" of rainfall in the Retalhuleu area during the period when the airstrip was being extended. The Chief of WH/4 Support said in fact, "the resident engineer is to be commended for the excellent performance of a difficult task." 15/

invasion. He then leaked the word that he was ac-
cepting offers of Cuban exiles in Guatemala to assist his country in its defense against a Castro
attack. All of these activities were being carried
on directly between the President of Guatemala and
the Agency's representatives in the field. The
Department of State, if informed of the GOG support
for JMATE, chose to appear ignorant of any involvement of the US Government.

Beginning in early August of 1960, Guatemala
Air Force B-26's and P-51's flew to all parts of
the country to provide additional support for the
cover story; and as Ydigoras had indicated in the
earlier part of the month, joint Army/Air maneuvers
began in the San Jose, Retalhuelu, and Champerico
areas to give further support to the story that the
increase in training activity was related to improv-
ing the status of the GOG's own military. To insure
the security of the area where the Agency activities
were centered, the newspapers and the public were
advised that they should not trespass in the training
areas because live ammunition was going to be

employed in the exercises. 16/*

The President of Guatemala was interested in doing more than simply providing a cover story for the Agency activities. Throughout the period prior to the invasion -- and even through the course of the invasion -- he or his chief spokesman, Roberto Alejos, made it quite clear on numerous occasions that they would be willing, indeed were anxious, to see Guatemalan Army and Air Force personnel actively participate in the operations against Castro's Cuba. As early as September 1960 when the first resupply overflight was being planned, Alejos and the Defense Minister of Guatemala were in serious discussion with Carl Jenkins, the COB of the ground training base, JMTRAV, about the possibility of using some Guatemalan personnel as either PDO's or assigning a counterpart Guatemalan Air Force crew to the C-54

---

* It is possible that this training was made possible, in part at least, by the 5,000 pounds of small arms and perhaps as much as 100,000 pounds of machine guns, ammunition, and rockets that CIA provided to the GOG at this time. 17/

that would be used in the overflight. 18/* The pros-
pect of utilizing Guatemalan personnel in addition
to the Cubans appeared attractive to Agency personnel
in the field, but it created negative responses from
Headquarters.

Sounding in one instance very much like a reply
originated from the Department of State, the Headquarters response to a [   ] request that a Guatemalan
cadre be infiltrated with the Cuban teams read: "Negative ... Possibility adverse political repercussions
too great to justify this action." 19/ The enthusiasm
in Guatemala also went beyond those immediately in
charge of the government. In October 1960 pending
a Guatemalan congressional investigation of activities

---

* An odd feature about the cable from [   ]
to Headquarters with Ydigoras's request was the following query: "Do you have Cuban crew selected? Would
they come from air group already in Guatemala?" This
would appear to be the long way around to get an
answer to the question and may reflect the incipient
antipathy between the WH/4 contingent at JMTRAV and
the DPD elements at the air base at Retalhuleu which
would later lead to harsh words and bitter recrimina-
tions that would only be solved -- and then in part --
by the DDP, Richard M. Bissell. As nearly as can be
determined, Carl Jenkins was the first COB at JMTRAV,
serving from early September until 9-10 December 1960. 18a/

at Retalhuleu, the principal political opponent of Ydigoras Fuente, Jose Cruz Salazar, who was scheduled to testify before the Congress about the air base, was briefed by Alejos and Ydigoras concerning their support for Project JMATE. Upon completion of this briefing, Guatemala cabled Headquarters that Cruz

> enthusiastically endorses effort and will assist provide cover for project before Congress. Also feels it advisable to have picked Guat in project. In turn, he said in two days he can easily raise an extra hundred who would be willing to fight against Castro and communism. 20/

By way of showing some appreciation to the GOG for its support, the Agency provided numerous name traces at the request of Alejos or Ydigoras -- name traces which turned up Castro agents in Guatemala or indicated legitimate Cuban defectors who wished to enter Guatemala. 21/ CIA assisted in having reported sightings of submarines of unknown origin off the west coast of Guatemala checked out -- submarines suspected of carrying arms or bringing pro-Castro guerrillas to Guatemala. In one instance ⬜ suggested that Headquarters fabricate a photo of a Soviet submarine supposedly off the Guatemalan coast. ⬜ said the photo could be placed in the Guatemalan press, and suggested "may be good way greeting Khrushchev on arrival UN." 22/*

It was also during the early period of initiation of activities in Guatemala that the Agency accommodated the request of President Ydigoras for about 20,000 rounds of 20mm anti-aircraft ammunition valued at about $30,000. The ammunition was to be used for training of AA gun crews, both as part of the cover and diversion from JMADD/JMTRAV activities and also as an actual part of the Guatemalan defense program against incursions of Cuban aircraft over their east coast. 23/

Relations with the GOG and its representatives were not all sweetness and light. A couple of annoying problems which came up in the early fall of 1960 concerned air operations, and the key figure, as in most of the disputes between the Agency and the GOG, was Roberto Alejos. In one instance he was exceedingly upset by the change in an incoming aircraft schedule, and Guatemala cabled Headquarters to insist -- again,

---

* CNO actually had P2V's sweeping the Pacific coast of Guatemala during the period 14-18 October 1960 in an attempt to locate a reported Soviet submarine -- with no luck.

apparently -- that last minute changes in flight schedules were unacceptable to Alejos and that if he could
not be given 24 hour notice of planned flights, then
schedules should be revised in order to accommodate
Alejos's demand. 24/ Some preliminary discussions
between the Agency's representatives in Guatemala and
the Thompson Cornwall Company (the construction company
responsible for the improvements of the Retalhuleu
airfield) over the question of providing cover for
the Agency's PBY came to naught when Alejos pointed
out the numerous difficulties which would attend the
attempts to cover the aircraft commercially. Alejos
noted that it would be much simpler to bring the PBY
in black, or chartered in his name, rather than to
attempt to use it under commercial cover. 25/

The problem of aircraft maintenance posed a
more serious question in terms of both cover and diplomatic relations with Guatemala. In the early summer
of 1960 negotiations had been undertaken with a Costa
Rican aircraft maintenance organization known as SALA.
The Development Projects Division, (DPD) which was
in charge of air operations for JMATE had initiated
the contacts with SALA through

[   ], a [   ] corporation which was Agency
controlled. For cover purposes it was owned by two
members of the FRD. Agency employees in key positions
in the company could monitor its activities and conduct
necessary business. The B-26 and C-46 aircraft for
use in the JMATE project were nominally to be sold
to the FRD by [   ] which, in turn, would
support the cover that the aircraft at JMADD belonged
to the Guatemalan Government. [   ] would
negotiate with SALA for maintenance of the "Guatemalan"
aircraft. All of this, of course, to involve ferrying
of B-26's from CONUS into Guatemala black, removing
and replacing of GOG insignia on aircraft as they
might move from Guatemala to Costa Rica where SALA
had its principal maintenance base, and generally
conducting operations in such a manner as to provide
viable cover. 25a/

By mid-September however, no agreement had yet
been reached. A few days prior to the time that the
DPD representatives planned to close the final agreement with SALA, a dispute arose between DPD and WH/4/PM.
The question concerned an apparent DPD attempt to go
it alone in the negotiations with SALA. The upshot

was that a SALA representative arrived in Guatemala City accompanied by the Costa Rican ambassador. The two Costa Ricans had then visited various Guatemalan officials seeking information about a damaged C-46 which DPD anticipated that SALA would be called on to repair. DPD planned to have the SALA representative, who had never been cleared by the Agency, visit the JMADD site. This visit was denied, and, in addition, Joseph Langan, Chief, WH/4 Security, in his memorandum on the incident stated:

> In view of the fact that relations between Guatemala and Costa Rica are apparently in a rather strained state at this time, these inquiries have resulted in placing the JMADD activities in an embarrassing situation relative to the Guatemalan government and in our dealings with various officials of said government ... Had the Guatemalan government been aware of the need for aircraft mechanics, this need might possibly have been filled from within Guatemala and obviated the necessity for bringing the SALA Corporation into the JMADD activity and, as a by-product, considerably reduced the expense of such activities. 26/

The maintenance contract between the Agency and SALA was never put into force because it got into these very sensitive political areas. 26a/

Because he played such a significant role in the Agency's relationship with his government, a special word should be said here about Roberto Alejos who was Ydigoras's alter ego in practically all matters concerning the Agency's Guatemala program. Alejos was informed on even the most minute details -- or if he was not informed, he let it be known that he was dissatisfied, displeased, and disagreeable. Where on the one hand he was almost solely responsible for covering the death of the first Cuban trainee, Carlos Rafael Santanya, whose dog tag number would be used to identify the exiles as the 2506 Brigade, on other occasions Alejos could behave as though he, rather than the Agency, were in charge of the training operation in Guatemala. With reference to the accidental death of the Brigade trainee, a cable from Guatemala to Headquarters noted that after the recovery of the body, the autopsy, and the burial, that:

> Alejos moved quickly to cover incident with local officials, from Governor down to adjoining finca manager. Thank God they all belong Government Party and he can control them. Believe total costs ops gifts no more than $1,000. 27/

In the early part of October 1960, Alejos was one of the principals in a potentially explosive incident which could have had serious repercussions, including possible loss of Guatemalan and US lives and the closing out of the training bases in Guatemala. The unfortunate situation seems to have occurred, in part at least, because of the inability of Agency personnel to communicate in Spanish with their Guatemalan hosts. Col. Antonio Batres had requested permission to enter the JMADD signal center in order to transmit a message. Batres was not only Chief of Guatemalan Air Force operations, he was also the personal pilot of President Ydigoras. The Agency officer in charge of the communications center had delayed Col. Batres a moment in order to secure sensitive materials in the area. According to the report to Headquarters, Batres thought that he was being denied access to the commo facilities which he apparently had utilized previously; and he departed the scene, only to return again with Roberto Alejos, half a dozen Guatemalan soldiers, and the commander of the Guatemalan security guard at JMADD. Alejos also was told that he would have to wait for a few minutes while the area was made secure -- at which pcint Alejos, accompanied by the commander of the Guatemalan guard unit and Batres, forced his way into the signal center and informed the Agency officer that he was under arrest.

Prior to, and in anticipation of, Alejos's return and the probability of a forced entry, the JMADD security officer had informed the communications officer that such an event would probably occur and that no resistance to Alejos should be made. Fortunately in the ensuing discussions between Alejos and the Agency's representatives, the situation was sorted out -- despite Alejos' angry statements that it was his intention to close down the communications activity in order to bring the number of negative aspects of the operation to the attention of "the big boys in Washington." 28/

There were, however, no repercussions nor security breaks resulting from this incursion by the Guatemalans into the commo center. The communications officer whom Alejos had declared to be "under arrest" was never technically arrested and, by way of apology, Alejos invited the officer to his home as a dinner guest.

D. Quid Pro Quos

Alejos's displays of temper may have had a less than subtle influence on subsequent negotiations with the Agency's representatives in Guatemala. Shortly after the foregoing incident, Chief, WH/4 (Jake Esterline) requested authority to obligate $150,000 for compensation to property owners in the area of the Retalhuleu air base for damages resulting from renovation of the airfield. Seventeen kilometers of roadway were reportedly "damaged considerably" when used as an access road to Roberto Alejos's finca, and repair on the seventeen kilometers was set at $100,000 -- plus an additional $50,000 to pay for rock taken from the river on property owned by one Señor Ralda on 5 acres of his property. 29/ Following Headquarters authorization of the payments to Alejos and Ralda, [   ] went to Headquarters with a cable on 4 Nov 1960 reading:

> 1. Payment of the $50,000 has to be made to Ralda immediately upon preparation and delivery of the local legal documents, as this Alejos understanding, and he had made the commitment to Ralda.
> 2. Operational activities and liaison with high Guat government officials would have been seriously affected, and the

- 24 -

success of the project materially jeopardized if payment is delayed. 3. Copies of legal documents will be forwarded Headquarters with the receipt. 30/

Despite the fact that the $100,000 was supposed to make the finca roadway and the 17 kilometers passable during the rainy season, an engineering report indicated that the steep grade was washing out the ballast and the road would need to be paved. Thompson-Cornwall, the engineering outfit which had restored Retalhuleu, had given an estimate of $185,000 to do the job. Alejos had tried to raise the difference between the $100,000 Headquarters had approved and the total contract price, but had been unable to do so. A cable of 25 Nov 60 from Guatemala indicated that _____ might be able to make a deal with Alejos for less than the full contract price and requested that he be authorized to offer a maximum of $130,000. The message to Headquarters ended with the standard plea that the negotiation be authorized as the matter was extremely delicate and could cause embarrassment to the project. An outgoing cable from the Director on 26 Nov 60 authorized ____ to negotiate up to $130,000 if that proved to be necessary; and the releasing officer for the cable was the DDP, Richard M. Bissell. 31/

In addition to these sums approved for payment to Alejos, other legitimate expenses the Agency incurred were for the use of Ydigoras's aircraft and for repaving and maintenance of the La Suiza airstrip on Alejos's property -- a total of $32,000. 32/ Alejos's various claims appear to have been legitimate expenses incurred under the terms of the open-ended oral contract·which had been in effect since the initiation of the project in Guatemala. Despite the failure of Alejos to sign documents for using an alias identity -- John Black -- or his failure to execute a written contract,   wrote that:

> JMATE does feel morally and legally obligated to reimburse Alejos for any expenses he incurs in his efforts for the Project if he submits a claim for reimbursement. It is on this basis that the relationship with Alejos now stands. To sum up the relationship between the Agency and Alejos, there has been no discussion of payment of salary or other monetary benefits. Alejos expects to be reimbursed for any expenses incurred in behalf of the Agency, and the Agency, to maintain its self respect and relationship with the Subject, is committed to pay for such expenses. 33/

Oral agreements notwithstanding, there is evidence that Alejos tried to take advantage of the situation on a number of occasions. As early as August 1960, for example, Alejos's brother-in-law, an engineer was proposed for a contract of $1,000 per month for work related to the development of the JMTRAV training site; and in January 1961, or shortly prior to January Alejos had proposed that Agency transport aircraft flying between Guatemala and Florida be used to carry shrimp to the United States. The numerous difficulties attendant upon such an operation were sufficient to cool this proposal, but far more pressure was exerted by Alejos during the period shortly before the invasion in an attempt to get the Agency to help him sell his coffee crop -- presumably because his participation in project activities had forced him to miss numerous opportunities to obtain the best price for his coffee. The Agency found an export agent in the US for Alejos, but the coffee sales were to be within the Guatemalan quota. 34/*

---

* How such relationships would be regarded in light of the investigative morality of the mid-1970's, is a moot point. At a time that the Bay of Pigs was being planned, the activities which now might seem
(footnote continued on following page)

E. November Revolt -- Policy Makers vs Pragmatists

For all practical purposes, the voice of the US
Government in Guatemala during the months when the
ground and air training bases -- JMTRAV and JMADD,
respectively -- were being established was that of
the Central Intelligence Agency. Agency training
programs were developed with the full and complete
cooperation of the President of Guatemala, his principal spokesman, Roberto Alejos, and other high GOG
officials. Such interest as the Department of State
evidenced in the affairs of Guatemala were concerned
principally with embarrassments that might result
from Cuban charges in the OAS or in the UN relating
to US support for Cuban exiles training in the Guatemalan area. By mid October of 1960 this point was
causing some consternation to Assistant Secretary of
State, Thomas Mann. 35/ From this time forward until
his replacement as Assistant Secretary of State for
American Republican Affairs, Mann was the Agency's

---

prejudicial were unquestionably necessary in view of
the fact that CIA was forced to use the Guatemalan
training sites. The Agency's preference for the use
of CONUS facilities for the training had been continu-
ously denied.

principal protagonist in the Department of State.

Despite this, however, he was a man who, in retro-

spect at any rate, was held in the highest regard

by both Richard Bissell, the DDP, and Jake Esterline,

Chief, WH/4.*

While Tom Mann would continue to be embroiled

in the Agency's relations with Guatemala, the United

_____

* In an Oral History Interview with the author in the
fall of 1975, Esterline had the following comments to
make about Mr. Mann:

    If you discussed a project in general
terms and he didn't like it, he would tell
you, but if you could bring him around
to the point where he said, "well, go a-
head and do it, but be damn sure that you
do it all out," that would be the end of
it. I think he was one of these who felt
that the prestige of the United States was
getting very thin in the hemisphere -- in
the sense of relating it to our gunboat
diplomacy days ... when we could of sort
of rape the lock and there would be no
problem with it. I think that he felt
that the odds of being able to put everything into it were very slim; but, again,
when he finally realized what the alterna-
tives were, he finally said, "Well, if this
is it, then let's do that plan, and let's
go the whole way on it." I had many go-
arounds with Tom on something until I
finally got him to agree, or he said,
"I am not going to agree." In this case
he finally agreed. No, it would be very
hard to fault Tom on the thing. 36/

States ambassador to Guatemala, John J. Muccio, who
preferred a back seat with regard to all activities
concerning the Cuban Brigade, was also going to be
forced into an active role in at least one event where
the Agency played the key role -- the preservation
of the Ydigoras presidency in November 1960. As
early as July of 1960, Ydigoras expressed to _____
_____ his fear that the *Partido General Trabajo*
and the *Partido Unidad Revolucionario* could possibly
overthrow his administration. With this in mind,
Ydigoras had discussed with _____ and Carl
Jenkins the possibility of forming a multi-national
force composed principally of anti-communists from
all parts of the world, including Guatemala and
other Latin American countries. As part of this
program, Roberto Alejos had suggested to ____ and
Jenkins that Guatemalan volunteers be trained as a
part of the JMATE operation. While the field was
favorably disposed to undertake this sort of training for the Guatemalans, no progress was made with
Headquarters on the plan. 37/*

_____

* In fact, Ydigoras and his Cabinet had decreed --
and the Congress had approved -- a 30 day state of
(footnote continued on following page)

By mid October 1960, the internal situation in
Guatemala had worsened, and Ydigoras was pressing
hard on Washington for loans and grants-in-aid to
assist him in maintaining control. The GOG faced a
financial crisis -- salaries had been cut, people
were unemployed, and the Leftists were making strong
inroads in the political life of the country. A
general strike had been called, and this posed a
possible threat to the overthrow of the Ydigoras
government. "Reports of varying reliability" suggested that Castro might be supplying funds to and
training cadres of anti-Ydigoras groups in Guatemala
in an attempt both to oust Ydigoras and, consequently,
put an end to Guatemalan support for the Cuban training program. The situation had become so serious
that by the end of October and the early part of
November JMADD had completed preparations for a quick
evacuation of all the aircraft and all station personnel

---

seige on 19 July 1960. Carl Jenkins, assigned to
WH/4/PM, was providing operational guidance to ____
prior to assuming his job as COB TRAV. In September
1960, Ernest W. Sparks was named Chief, JMATE activities
in Guatemala and thus became the adviser to _____
_____ on ops plans. 37a/

to France Field in Panama. Ydigoras himself was facing strong congressional opposition from those who refused to believe that he had not permitted the use of Guatemalan territory for the training of the anti-Castro Cuban group.

How desperate the situation appeared to the GOG was noted in a cable from Headquarters to Guatemala:

> JMARC principal Department of State contact told [Gerard] Droller that Alejos [presumably Ambassador Alejos] had informed President Eisenhower of Guat plan stage Cuban invasion Guat. According this plan, it is intended for number of Cubans land Guat beach and dig for arms caches ostensibly placed there by Castro agents. "Invading Cubans" would be apprehended by Guats and brought to trial. Trial proceedings would be extremely fair and sentences extremely light. Ydigoras desires contrast Guat application justice with that of Castro. Intended that the entire operation be bloodless and without shooting. 38/

It was not clear whether the "invaders" were to be volunteers from among the troops in training at JMTRAV, but before any such operation could take place, a real crisis broke in Guatemala.

On 13 November 1960 an emergency cable from JMADD was received in Headquarters at 0931 (Washington time), stating that Roberto Alejos had arrived at the

MADD base to tell the Agency representatives that
various cities, including Guatemala City, were having
"minor skirmishes with communist elements." At this
time, Alejos made a request that MADD "be prepared
to participate in show of strength in form of fly-
overs" and it was the plan of the Acting Chief of
JMADD to comply with Alejos's request pending Headquarters approval. 39/ The American Embassy's initial
message was received in the Department at 1234 hours
(Washington time), and said "some kind of uprising"
in Guatemala City had been aborted. 39a/

Within a few hours of the first announcement of
the revolt, there began a rash of emergency cable
traffic among Guatemala City, JMADD, and Headquarters
that continued for the next three to four days. Almost
immediately, for example, key Agency personnel in
Guatemala were hit with requests for support and
assistance from the Ydigoras government. One of the
first requests came from the Minister of Defense,
Rubin Gonzales Sigui who, fearful that the revolt was
being directed and sponsored by Cuban elements, asked
that the US provide surveillance for enemy ships which
might be oprating between Cuba and Puerto Barrios --

one of the principal centers of the revolt. In response to this request, which also was supported by the US ambassador in Guatemala City, the Navy authorized two P2V aircraft to survey the area as far south as Panama and, in addition, assigned a destroyer to patrol the Gulf of Honduras area.* 39b/ The charge that the revolt was Castro backed would be repeated throughout the period of the revolution, but no evidence was ever found to indicate that it was anything other than an internal uprising of dissident Guatemalans, principally elements of the Army. In fact, before the revolutionary episode came to a conclusion, the Political and Psychological warfare unit of WH/4 was to suggest that if legitimate evidence was not found to implicate Castro, that such evidence be manufactured to show that the basis for the revolution wàs in fact from Fidel Castro and his coterie.

During the course of the first day's action, the Cuban forces in training at JMTRAV were alerted to prepare for any contingency. The Guatemalan troops which had been used as part of the cover and security

---

* Unsourced comments in the following paragraphs are based on cables reproduced in Appendix 1, Guatemalan Revolt, 13 November 1960: Miscellaneous Cables.

forces in the TRAV and MADD areas were called to service by Ydigoras, and the Agency's C-46 aircraft out of JMADD participated in transporting these troops to Guatemala City. There was considerable concern about the fact that this left only one C-46 at the Retalhuleu airfield, and this would be insufficient should an emergency evacuation of the Cuban Brigade and Agency personnel be required. Headquarters directed, however, that air transport support continue to be given to the Ydigoras government. An additional problem presented almost immediately to JMATE was a GOG request for large amounts of ordnance to replace expenditures from the first day's strafing and rocket attacks by Guatemalan Air Force B-26's on various points which had fallen to the rebel forces. The Guatemalan government requested, among other ordnance, components for manufacturing napalm bombs; but this request was rejected for technical reasons.

Requests from the field went to Headquarters for the standby of additional B-26's that might be needed by MADD and for C-54 flights to bring in small arms and ammunition. The Chief of Air operations at JMADD, Major Billy B. Campbell, had been to Headquarters

for meetings with DPD and was visiting [ ],
Eglin Air Force Base en route back to MADD at the
outbreak of the revolt.* At one point it was planned
that Campbell and another B-26 pilot would make an
emergency flight to MADD with the bomb bays of the
B-26's loaded with ammunition and arms. By mid afternoon on 13 November, [ ], Lt. Col. Frank
Egan, who would soon (9/10 December 1960) take charge
of the TRAV base, and Lt. Col. Quentin V. Earl, who
in the absence of Billy Campbell was proceeding to
the MADD base as commanding officer, went forward to
Headquarters with a GOG request to use JMATE's B-26's
and US pilots if they would volunteer to fight for
the Ydigoras government.** MADD also indicated that

---

* [   ]

** In an Oral History interview with the author on
15 June 76, Lt. Col. Billy B. Campbell (USAF, Ret.)
offered a somewhat different version of the GOG
approach to JMADD. Campbell stated that:

> Alejos had been at the base just prior
> to my getting back down and had Guat
> troops and had threatened to take over
> the base -- JMADD -- and take over the
> aircraft and use his own pilots to quell
> the invasion which was coming up through
> Puerto Barrios and Honduras. 39c/
>   (footnote continued on following page)

Ydigoras would like to use the JMTRAV Cubans -- the
majority of whom had volunteered to fight for Guatemala -- to help put down the revolt. As the first
day wore on, the situation of the Guatemalan government became increasingly difficult. Ydigoras ordered
a 30-day state of siege and called an emergency session
of Congress. The rebel forces were gaining more ground,
literally and figuratively.

Apparently failing to receive an answer from
Headquarters concerning the use of US pilots and Cuban
troops, [   ] cabled Headquarters shortly before 0300 hours (Washington time) on 14 November 1960
with a request from Ernie Sparks and Col. Egan for
permission to commit 218 Cuban volunteers from JMTRAV
as airborne infantry for an assault landing at the
Puerto Barrios air base at dawn. In addition, they
also requested permission to utilize MADD B-26's
piloted by US personnel -- volunteers again -- to

Although the cable traffic fails to mention
this incursion by Alejos, it is verified by an eye-
witness who was present in the communications room
at Retalhuleu when Alejos forced himself into the
secure area. This witness recalled Headquarter's
instructions to cooperate with Alejos and also the
authorization for Seigrist and Beale to fly strikes
against the rebels in Puerto Barrios. 39d/

support the attack. The reason for the use of US

B-26 pilots was given as follows:

> Due fact Guat pilots have had no prac-
> tice this type op and Cuban pilots have
> not yet participated in combined air/
> ground exercises plus need for precise
> timing and coordination air strike with
> air assault landing, request authority
> use US volunteer pilots to insure success
> this op.

> Request authority use one AEDEPOT
> volunteer with each assault transport
> aircraft to provide best leadership
> available. 40/*

The Headquarters reaction to this request is

best explained in the words of the then Deputy Direc-

tor of Plans, Richard M. Bissell who said:

> I remember with some vividness that I
> was called up by the Watch Officer at
> about 2:30 in the morning and a cable had
> come in, I think from Egan, and Ydigoras
> had asked to borrow some of the Brigade
> to put down an uprising in Puerto Barrios.
> Egan wanted an answer within an hour or
> something of that kind. I did, at that
> hour in the morning, get in touch with
> Tom Mann; but I could get no decision out
> of Tom Mann. He said he couldn't possibly
> act on a matter of that kind until he could

---

* AEDEPOTS were defectors from the USSR who had been
trained initially by the Agency for various types of
_____ operations _____ . Because their
primary mission was phasing out, some 26 of them
volunteered and were used as training officers at
JMTRAV. See also, pp. 66-67 of this volume.

see the Secretary in the morning. So
here again, you have Ydigoras levying a
request on an Agency representative
locally, under circumstances and with a
time schedule that, as it turned out,
made effective reference to the State
Department just impossible. The State
Department was not equipped to decide
something like that within an hour. ...
I know that I sent a cable to Egan saying
"Yes" on my responsibility; and my reasons
for doing that -- very definitely at the
time -- were that I didn't think that decision ought to be left to Egan. 41/

There seems to have been some confusion as to

what actually happened following the request which

Mr. Bissell approved. The initial cable reporting

the action stated simply that:

> Upon Ydigoras's instructions through
> Alejos, aircraft and troops launched on
> schedule. However, when planes at Puerto
> Barrios, order countermanded as it dis-
> covered majority rebels had evacuated base
> during night. All aircraft and TRAV
> troops returned JMADD. 42/

On 17 November however, in an after action report it

was stated:

> MADD B-26's commenced airstrike against
> Puerto Barrios air base at 0607 hours local,
> strafing area with rockets and .50 cal.
> As first C-46 started to land, B-26's strafed
> in front landing C-46. C-46 made successful
> landing encountering sporadic small arms
> fire. Cuban trainees aboard aircraft re-
> turned fire through ports during landing.
> Recall order given before C-46 completed
> landing. Therefore, pilot did 180 degree

turn and took off immediately and all
C-46's and B-26's returned directly to
MADD. 43/

The most accurate story of the air operation
mounted by the Agency, however, comes from the principal eye witness to the actual operation against Puerto
Barrios, C. W. (Connie) Seigrist, who had initially
ferried one of the B-26's to Guatemala from the Agency's
operations in the Far East, Seigrist has written:

> I believe the Guatemalan Army Colonel
> who was in charge of our base informed us
> of the revolt. This was late in the after-
> noon [of 13 November 60]. I offered my
> services, if needed, in support of President
> Ydigoras. So did some of the Cubans. We
> felt what we were working for would all go
> down the tubes if the revolt was successful
> and we were exposed. Late at night, our
> offer was accepted. The Guatemalan Air Force
> refused to participate.
>
> I flew a B-26 with a Cuban pilot-observer
> named Crespo (he was lost later flying a
> B-26 at the Bay of Pigs). I strafed and
> rocketed the airfield at Puerto Barrios to
> soften the field for the C-46's that were
> carrying the Cuban troops who were to
> repluse a revolt. The Guatemalan Air Force
> Colonel, Antonio Batres, asked me later to
> fly cover for Guatemala army troops who
> were flown into some airfields in the
> mountains to counterattack a part of the
> revolt. Although I flew cover, no close
> support action was required of me. I flew
> alone. Also, later Col. Batres asked me
> to patrol the entire southwest portion
> along the coast of Guatemala and to fire

> into any grouping of people or vehicles.
> I patrolled most of the day, stopping to
> refuel once, but no action was required
> as there wasn't a soul or vehicle in sight.
> I flew alone. 44/*

Among other details provided by Seigrist was the fact

that two B-26's were involved in the Puerto Barrios

action, the second being flown by W. H. Beale, who

also had flown a B-26 in from the Far East. Seigrist

flew a total of four sorties, including one to Puerto

Barrios, one in the mountains, and two along the coast.

Except for the operation in the mountains when he re-

fueled at Guatemala City National Airport, Seigrist

confined his flights to Retalhuleu. With reference

to the actual strike, Seigrist noted as follows:

> Our targets were restricted by Col.
> Batres in the Puerto Barrios sortie.

---

* There is support for Seigrist's comments re the
Guatemalan Air Force in the cable traffic. Cables to
Washington from both [   ] and the Ambassador indicated that the Air Force officers were unhappy about
both using the Cubans and shooting their fellow Guatemalans. In a meeting of the Special Group, Livingston
Merchant of State regarded this matter "with extreme
gravity, commenting that it might well lead President
Ydigoras to withdraw permission for us to continue in
Guatemala." 45/ Inasmuch as Ydigoras had already decided that his control of the government depended on
support from JMADD (and JMTRAV) Merchant's fears
seem unwarranted.

Some of the airfield buildings were supposed to be holding hostages, but the field
proper with its supply sheds and such were
pulverized. We strafed ditches, bushes,
or anything where someone could find cover
close enough to the runway to harass the
C-46's that were to land with the Cuban
troops. We never were informed of KIA or
wounded counts. We did hear that a couple
of Americans on the ground watched Bill and
I at a safe distance and reported that we
did a tremendous job -- whatever that might
mean.

Three C-46's were involved. [They were]
flown by Cubans. One C-46 landed. As it
was rolling to a stop, the Cuban troops
started firing out the doors and escape
hatches. The pilot thought he had landed
in a trap and continued to take off without ever having come to a stop. They refused (all three C-46's) to land after that
and returned to Retalhuleu with all other
troops still aboard.

I would guess around 100 troops were
involved. I can only estimate at what I
saw. As to Agency trainers -- here, again,
time has slipped my memory -- but I believe
their American Commander was on one of the
C-46's, but not the C-46 that landed. He
was still the same Commander for the Bay
of Pigs.*

---

* This is a reference to Lt. Col. Frank Egan, the PM
trainer. Egan's version of the incident is somewhat
different than Seigrists. In his testimony to the
Taylor Committee Egan said:

. President Ydigoras requested that we
make an airborne landing, which we did.
I was in command of the outfit. Washington gave us permission to do this, but I
operated under the Mission Chief in Guatemala.

(footnote continued on following page)

I personally flew a total of around 15
hours on the four sorties. This covered
a two day period. My last sortie in the
late afternoon on the coast of the second
day [15 Nov 60] ended at MADD. I was informed that the revolt was over. I heard
that Col. Batres had flown to Puerto Barrios
and was negotiating with the ones in charge
of the revolt. I was not privileged to
find out the results of the revolt, but it
was over. I believe the Guatemalan Air
Force cancelled our flights when they
informed us of Col. Batres' actions ... I
did accept my orders at the time and did
support Col. Batres' command, but my bosses
were Americans; and I would have responded
to their orders. None were given after
their first permission for me to follow
Col. Batres. 46/

Jacob D. Esterline, Chief of JMARC project had

some subsequent conversation with the Americans who

were mentioned in Seigrist's report. In discussions

where he had suggested that the B-26's operating

Inasmuch as Egan did not give any specifics about de-
planing his troops, both he and Seigrist could be
technically correct.

The Deputy Chief of DPD claimed that 216 Cuban
troops "were committed to Puerto Barrios airstrip at
0600 hours on 14 November. If it is possible, these
troops will have to be evacuated if the situation
worsens." Once again, however, the language is vague
enough to be true, since the referenced evacuation of
the Cuban troops does not specify that they were to
be evacuated from Puerto Barrios. There is no argument, of course, that they "were committed to Puerto
Barrios airstrip," but only in what amounted to a
touch-and-go landing. 45a/

against Puerto Barrios had been flown by Guatemalan
pilots, Jake

> was challenged several times by people
> from the United Fruit Company who were
> there at Puerto Barrios at the time, and
> they said "look, we have been living a-
> round Guatemala for years and we have
> never seen Guatemalan pilots fly or shoot
> with the precision that these fellows
> shot. They didn't kill anybody." (Any-
> body that they weren't supposed to kill,
> I guess is the way to put it.) There
> wasn't a stray bullet anywhere, they
> strictly hit military targets. But
> there was a case of a green light from
> State Department, and then they said
> they didn't mean it. It was academic,
> because it was done. 47/*

---

* Esterline's additional comments are indicative of
the confusion that one faces in trying to sort out
details of the Bay of Pigs, 16 years after the event.
In contrast to Bissell's previously noted remarks
with reference to the cable requesting permission
to act in response to Ydigoras's request, Jake noted
that:

> We got this urgent call requesting the
> use of our troops. We got it, and we looked
> at it and didn't know what to do with it.
> We called State Department and said, "We
> suppose this is critical. The whole thing
> is going to pot." I suppose that it was
> Rubottom or somebody at that level over
> there, that we called. They said "Well, I
> guess you had better give him what he wants."
> So we gave him what he wanted, and that
> was about the time that it was in motion;
> and we got a call back from State Depart-
> ment saying they'd checked, and they didn't
> mean it, but it was in motion at that point. 48/

When the critical request for assistance came
in from Egan, the operation -- per Mr. Bissell's decision -- was approved in an outgoing cable from
Washington shortly after 0500 hours on the morning
of 14 November and it was stated specifically that
only CAT pilots could be used -- if they volunteered. 49/*
Although the outgoing authorization indicated "we
concerned that Cuban troops being committed in advance of Guat troops, also feel part of the strike
force must be Guatemalan to offset stigma of attack
by foreign mercenaries," there is no indication that
Guatemalan troops were aboard the C-46's headed for
Puerto Barrios; and as Seigrist pointed out, he flew
the Puerto Barrios strike with a Cuban in the right
seat and presumably Beale also used a Cuban as his
co-pilot. 50/

In addition to the transport of Guatemalan and
Cuban troops by C-46's and the B-26 sorties, other
events also occupied those Agency personnel at JMADD
and JMTRAV. One of the most immediate was the GOG's

---

* This was to eliminate the possibility that any of
the Agency's USAF assignees at JMADD might be involved
in a shoot down or accident.

need for additional small arms and ammunition. During
the course of 14 November, there was a heavy exchange
of cable correspondence on this subject, with the ul-
timate plan being that C-124's would pick up materiel
from [   ] at [   ] and would deliver
the required submachine guns, ammunition for the submachine guns, and large quantities of .30 and .50
caliber ammunition to Eglin Air Force Base where it
would be picked up by two C-54's and flown down to
Retalhuleu air base. 50a/ The C-54 flights were
authorized to use USAF or [   ] contract air crews
(OSTIARIES) or any combination of these crews for the
deliveries. Flight plans and landing approaches to
Retalhuleu were given in great detail in the cable
traffic to insure that the materiel -- and personnel
-- arrived safely. Discussions concerning emergency
evacuation plans for the TRAV and MADD bases were
initiated with DOD representatives, and an emergency
signal plan was also prepared.* 50b/

---

* Emergency plans were for air evacuation of Project
personnel from Retalhuleu to France Field in the Panama
Canal Zone. Contingency planning in case of loss of
the airstrip at Retalhuleu called for surface transport
from TRAV and MADD to Champerico on the west coast and
transfer to small boats at that point for evacuation
(footnote continued on following page)

With this flurry of activity it is interesting
to note that it was more than 24 hours before Headquarters got around to giving its concurrence to
the assignment of Lt. Col. Earl as Chief of Base at
JMADD and Lt. Col. Egan as Acting Chief of Base at
JMTRAV. The Chief of the JMADD air operations, Billy
Campbell, who was up at Eglin Air Force Base when
the revolt broke out was off-again-on-again in terms
of his return to Retalhuleu. Before the close of
14 November, Campbell's orders had been changed back
to the original date and time of departure (15 November) and the plan to have him fly ammunition down to
MADD in a B-26 had been scrubbed. Before committing
any DPD aircraft Headquarters carefully inquired if
any "Guat air assets defected or been taken over by
rebels which [*sic*] can knock down JMCLEAR aircraft.
Are their [*sic*] any Guat areas to be avoided." 51/

About mid-day on 14 November 1960, Headquarters
informed Guatemala City that there had been a telecon

---

by vessels of the USN. Coincidental with possible
evacuation were discussions of alternative training
sites for the Cubans, including bases in the Z.I.,
or transfer to   training facility. 50c/

between Ambassador Muccio and Secretary of State

Christian Herter concerning use of the Cubans to

help quell the revolt. On this point Ambassador

Muccio would cable later:

> In justification Ydigoras attempted
> use last week must report that understand
> prior "Washington authorization" given to
> use trainees. I knew nothing their use
> until half hour prior Secretary's call.
> ... I sent message through ▯▯▯▯▯▯
> urging Ydigoras confine them to military
> bases and not operate out into civilian
> areas. 52/*

By mid-afternoon, a joint State/CIA message, originated

by C. Tracy Barnes, ADDP/A, was sent to ▯▯▯▯▯▯

stressing that if there were any Cuban trainees at or

near Puerto Barrios they should be recalled to Retalhuleu

This cable also suggested the possibility that all the

Cuban trainees might be removed from Guatemala (this

would be an on-going subject of speculation until the

close out of the revolt). 53/

Even as the joint message was going forward,

Headquarters was aware of the fact that the Cuban

---

* The admission by Muccio that he was unaware of the
fact that members of the Brigade -- to say nothing of
the B-26 sorties by Seigrist and Beale -- were being
airlifted to Puerto Barrios speaks poorly for the
Ambassador's awareness of the situation and indicates
that the Agency was playing it close to the vest vis-
a-vis Muccio.

troops had not been deplaned at Puerto Barrios; but the Department of State wanted to put into the official record that they were in opposition to using Cuban troops to support Ydigoras and that Guatemala should request the US to assist in preventing the importation of foreign arms or forces -- Cuban, that is -- into Guatemala. Following its request to the US, the Department wanted the GOG to ask formally for OAS action under the Rio Treaty.

The joint State/Agency message also asked that the field supply any information that could be discovered of Cuban involvement in the Guatemalan revolt and then it went on to walk the line between the possibility of Ydigoras's survival and Ydigoras's overthrow. Lest the record be unclear, [   ] was directed as follows:

> To avoid ambiguity the following actions are now authorized:
>
> A. Continued use of C-46's for troop movement and for other necessary transport. Assume pilots are either CAT or Cubans.
>
> B. Provide GOG with ammo and other materiel if, and only if, senior responsible GOG officer specifically requests such materiel; [   ] in consultation with Ambassador agrees that

need exists and transfer otherwise
proper.

C. Provide GOG with B-26 aircraft if,
    and only if, critical need exists,
    use likely give substantial advan-
    tage, and GOG can provide pilots.

In connection with any decision support
Ydigoras weigh possibility whether not
remote that rebels may not be left wing nor
anti-US, as active support [for Ydigoras]
under such circumstances could be undesir-
able. 53a/*

Before the afternoon (14 November) was over, a

cable from Headquarters went to all Latin American

stations alerting everyone to the possibility of

Cuban intervention in any of the Latin American coun-

tries. It warned:

As events unfold, keep in mind, we
want picture Castro "intervention" as
result clandestine subversion, money

---

* As already reported, "ambiguity" was not avoided --
Connie Seigrist has noted that he flew some 15 hours
in the course of two days, 14-15 November. According
to this message -- which was received at approximately
1400 hours Guatemalan time on 14 November -- Seigrist
technically should have been grounded. As Seigrist
reported, however, he was taking orders from Col.
Batres because no one had told him otherwise. Seigrist
continued to follow the initial orders that he had been
given to support Col. Batres's requests, and he stopped
flying missions when Guatemalan officers told him the
revolt had ended.

payments, arms traffic, illegal Cuban
Embassy participation, etc. and not give
false impression Cuban revolution "catch-
ing on" in popularity other WH countries.
Also use any pertinent news peg as occa-
sion mention continued shipments and training in use Soviet bloc arms including
artillery by Castro militia. 54/

By 16 November 1960, the revolt for all practical

purposes had come to an end. At that time there were

pockets of resistance reported in the area between

Puerto Barrios and Gualán, but no evidence had been

found which would support charges of Cuban involvement.

Before the conclusion of the fighting, however, Presi-

dent Ydigoras did request -- and received -- two of

the JMADD B-26's because the Guatemalan Air Force

B-26's had been shot up to the point where they were

in no condition to fly additional combat missions. As

a result of the unsettled situation in Guatemala, re-

cruitment of PM ground trainees for JMTRAV was suspended

until further notice, the B-26's were recalled to the

JMADD air base, and, for the moment, all Air National

Guard (ANG) and military assignees to MADD were con-

fined to the base.* During the course of the revolt

---

* It was reported to Headquarters that on the morning
of 15 Nov 60, four armorers from MADD had been briefly
detained by an "officer group" at the Guatemala City
airfield. The detainees probably were USAF military
assignees.

in Guatemala, Headquarters informed the base in Florida to "discourage" Tony Varona from sending any FRD volunteers into the Central American area; and Headquarters also rejected a request from the GOG to have Agency lie detector experts participate in interrogating the captured rebel prisoners. As an alternative, [____] was told to provide guidance to the GOG to hire a commercial firm to participate in the interrogation of the prisoners.*

F. Minor Skirmishes: Inter- and Intra-Agency

In addition to the two B-26's JMADD supplied to the Guatemalan Air Force during the course of the revolt, upon completion of the revolt, it was recommended by the Agency, by the Air Attache, and by the Chief of the US Air Mission in Guatemala that eight new B-26's be procured for the Guatemalan Air Force and that these be configured in a manner similar to the aircraft being operated out of the MADD base. Unfortunately, however, at this point in the game, the US Ambassador was "willing

_____

* See Appendix 1 for copies of cable traffic on the various items mentioned in the foregoing paragraph.

send recommendation only upon formal request from GOG and does not wish ask GOG unless first assured US Government willingness grant request if made." 55/*

Even as the revolt was being quelled, the US Ambassador was renewing his pleas for the Department to get behind the economic aid program he had been discussing with the GOG since the late spring. In fact in mid October 1960, Mr. Muccio had recommended that a loan and grant package totalling almost $13 million be approved. The requests were approved before the end of November, about the same time that the Department of State was expressing concern about the Agency's role in Guatemala. 56/ Headquarters requested:

> contact Ydigoras and ask him
> whether continued presence Cuban train-
> ees is placing undue strain on his
> government. One sector State at least
> contends their presence is unwarranted
> liability and strongly urging removal
> JMTRAV elements soonest. Ydigoras
> completely frank estimate urgently
> needed. 57/

"Immediate" said:

[Ydigoras's personal message] emphatically

---

* Delivery of the eight B-26's was never made to the Government of Guatemala.

stated that any speculation on above
matter is completely unfounded and that
he will back this project to the end.
Also recommends strengthening forces to
avoid failures. When action finally
taken we must be sure of success. 58/

It appears probable that the regional area of State

which was evincing concern was the office of American

Republic Affairs (ARA) directed by Assistant Secretary

Mann.*

---

* Although the author believes that State's perspi-
cacity during the BOP operation was limited by it's
extreme caution, there is nonetheless evidence to suggest the Department may have had reason to regard those
involved in the JMATE operation with some suspicion.
A cable of 30 November 1960 to [   ] of Central
America read as follows:

    1. CIA deliberately fomented leak by
    State of earlier fairly solid report re
    Cuban 'militiamen' flights over Guat which
    should be useful Guatemala in case against
    Cuba and should be played WH assets through-
    out area to prove Cuban aggression Central
    America.

    2. *Washington Evening Star*, 22 November
    and (better yet) *New York Times*, 24 November
    said Cuban recon flights with armed militia-
    men aboard occurred end October. In *Times*
    version several flights took place 29-31 Oc-
    tober, total 150 Cuban militiamen carried
    and fewer returned to Cuban airport than
    left. According *Star*, two Cuban plane num-
    bers were 601 and 631. (631 independently
    confirmed as Cuban recon plane which buzzed
    Swan Island 27 October. This fact now overt.)
    Attribution, both papers were 'diplomatic
    sources.' 59/

(footnote continued on following page)

The fact of long continuing support from the government of Guatemala showed in an incident of early December which also reflected some internal dissension between [   ] and the Chief of Base at JMTRAV. Colonel Egan had apparently arranged for an air reception and field training exercise for a group of Cuban trainees at the "finca San Jose" (probably the finca San Juan in the San Jose area) which was another of the properties Robert Alejos made available to the Agency; but somewhere in the process Egan had failed to clear the exercise with either [   ] or the local authorities -- military and civil -- in the area of the finca. The result being that:

> Airdrops attracted attention local secur-
> ity forces who appear considerably more
> alert and effective than in TRAV area.
> Night 7 December delegations from national
> police, military, and Army MP visited finca.
> Fortunately Alejos was visiting and ex-
> plained that no invasion in progress, only
> secret army maneuvers.

In his cable to headquarters reporting the incident, Chief of Base TRAV also had indicated that a planned

---

This particular cable is another of the relatively few concerning the JMATE operation which were released by Richard Helms as Chief of Operations, DDP.

increment in the number of trainees into the TRAV
area was reported to have gotten a negative response
from Alejos. 60/

But following receipt of his copy of the cable,
[   ] sent an OPIM to the director pointing
out that COB TRAV had failed to properly coordinate
his cable for, in truth, Alejos was reported to
have been "enthusiastic about additional 400 men in
training program" and, furthermore, according to
[   ], Alejos had taken a number of steps to place
additional facilities at the disposal of the incoming trainees, including additional housing and
the laying of a pipeline to insure that there would
be no shortage of water at JMTRAV. [   ] chewed on
COB TRAV for failure to coordinate because this
was the sort of thing which could lead to the break-
down of the cover story and embarrassment to the
GOG. [   ] message closed on the following note:

> [   ] wishes to make a matter of record
> for benefit COB's future action and DIR
> information the fact that COB's will not
> (repeat not) release cables to HQS on
> policy or political matters until sub-
> jects have been properly staffed out with
> [   ]. [   ] intends to relieve COB from

duty the next time this occurs. 61/*

G. The Special Forces Trainers -- Pragmatism and Patience

As mentioned in the introduction to the discussion
of the relations with Guatemala, a second episode involving the Agency in a unique situation with the GOG
concerned the use of US Army Special Forces personnel
to train the Cuban ground forces. Almost immediately
following Eisenhower's approval of the anti-Castro
program in March 1960, WH/4 faced the problem of acquiring trained personnel to instruct the cadre being prepared for small unit guerrilla warfare operations; and
later there were numerous difficulties in acquiring

---

* Unlike [   ] during the course of the activities related to the Bay of Pigs, [   ] was
very positively identified in all of the actions involving Agency personnel and he was particularly close
to the center of power with his relationships to
Roberto Alejos and President Ydigoras. While the
author has no way of knowing what Colonel Egan's reaction was to [   ] Billy Campbell indicated that
relations between [   ] and the air operations at JMADD
were also sometimes rather strained and that he, too,
had been threatened with removal [   ]. It is not
known, however, whether Campbell was referring to [   ]
or to [   ] who came in as [   ] in
December 1960 -- even though [   ] continued to [   ]
[   ] for Cuban ops from December until the collapse
of the invasion. Whoever made the threat, Campbell
said that he ran the JMADD air ops as instructed by
DPD not [   ]. 61a/

personnel for training the invasion force. Although
not without difficulty, small unit cadres were trained
at Fort Randolph in the Panama Canal Zone for infiltra-
tion, the establishment of commo activities, and sabotage.
With the move to Guatemala, it was obvious that additional trainers would be required; and as a result,
Chief JMATE worked very closely with Soviet Division,
particularly the Domestic Operations Base, to obtain
the services of the so-called "unofficial Americans"
who had been recruited by SB under the AEDEPOT program
to serve as trainers for the Cuban Brigade. Formal
arrangements between the Soviet Division and JMATE
were concluded in early September 1960. 62/ Despite
the fact that the AEDEPOT program had been initiated

a total of 21
agents and five staff personnel joined the JMATE project. The actual recruiting was run through the FRD
recruitment program headed by Juan Paula Argeo. The
WH representatives were introduced as US Government
officials sympathetic to the cause of the anti-Castro
Cubans. It was pointed out, however, that the US

Government could not officially sponsor or openly support the movement; and, therefore, these Americans
were working unofficially to assist the Cubans in
their search for volunteer instructors, cadre leaders,
and so on. As one report put it, "the cover story
didn't hold up well and the agents soon knew they
were working for the CIA; however, in almost all cases
the agents believed that Army intelligence had loaded
them to CIA and compartmentation was maintained." 63/

With the closeout of the Panama training activity
and the move to Guatemala and with the opening of the
JMTRAV activity and the increasing number of recruits,
the small number of Soviet Division assets who were
being used to train the Cubans were being spread too
thin; and JMATE turned to the United States Army
Special Forces for assistance. The problem of the
acquisition of the requisite number of Special Forces
training officers was the one which would involve
Chief, JMATE in a unique relationship with the GOG,
and would precipitate a lengthy, often acrimonious,
series of discussions which involved the Special
Group, the Department of State, the Department of
Defense, the Department of the Army, and even the

President of the United States himself, Dwight D. Eisenhower.

The Agency's request which was to touch off the brouhaha was initiated by Col. Jack Hawkins (USMC), Chief, WH/4/PM on 19 October 1960. After approval through the chain of command to the DDP was formalized (16 November 1960), then J. C. King, Chief, Western Hemisphere Division, prepared a memorandum for the Mobilization and Military Personnel Division (MMPD), Office of Personnel, CIA asking that 38 US Army Special Forces personnel be acquired for training JMARC assets in a foreign area. In his memorandum, Col. King noted that Captain Burns Spore, Office of Special Operations, Department of Defense had been informed about the requirement; but since no official action had yet been taken by DOD regarding the Special Forces personnel, MMPD was being asked to make it official.

At a subsequent meeting between representatives of WH/4 and Captain Spore, the DOD representative apparently got his back up about the lack of information that DOD -- in his opinion at any rate -- had about the Agency's operational plans against Cuba. Inasmuch as the Agency's request came about the same time that serious thought was being given to the possible removal of the Cuban trainees from Guatemala, the DOD representative was much concerned about the actual base at which it was intended to station the Special Forces trainers. Until this matter could be cleared up to the satisfaction of DOD, Captain Spore assumed the position that no further action would be taken with regard to the Special Forces personnel. Jake Esterline, Chief, JMATE, made a strong plea to the DOD representative based on the argument that the question about the actual site of the training activity was up in the air as a result of Department of State cautiousness; and Esterline expressed the opinion that as a result of State's greater interest in the program of economic strangulation of Cuba, the situation for the United States and for other Latin American governments friendly to the United States would grow increasingly desperate. He further suggested that the Department of Defense was being tainted by State's opposition rather than by realistic appraisal of the situation in Cuba, and he volunteered to brief senior DOD personnel at a time convenient to them. 64/

The question of the use of Special Forces personnel was brought before the Special Group in its meeting on 30 November, 5 December, and 8 December of 1960. From the 8 December meeting came the unique suggestion which Thomas Parrot, Executive Secretary for the Special Group, noted in the minutes of that meeting:

> Mr. Douglas [James H. Douglas, Deputy Secretary of Defense] went on to say that he is anxious to make the 38 trainers available but that the Army wants to have them as fully protected as possible. He, therefore, asked that CIA explore the situation further to see if the Government of Guatemala could not make a formal request for trainers from the DOD. Mr. Esterline said that he thought a secret agreement could be negotiated with President Ydigoras, but that it would not be feasible to have an open agreement of any kind. Mr. Mann expressed some fears about having anything in writing with Ydigoras because of his somewhat unsure tenure. He asked that this be taken up with him later. (At the later meeting referred to above, Mr. Mann agreed to a plan suggested by CIA whereby a secret agreement would be negotiated, but no signed copy would be in the hands of the GOG.) 65/

Following the suggestion that a secret agreement be negotiated with the government of Guatemala, plans were made for Jake Esterline to fly black into Guatemala to undertake negotiations with Ydigoras. The affair then became a comedy of near misses. It was anticipated that Roberto Alejos would be contacted prior to the meeting with Ydigoras to get the President's opinion on signing the proposed secret agreement. Unfortunately, however, Alejos was arriving in Washington about the time that Esterline was scheduled to land in Guatemala.*

With Esterline in Guatemala and Alejos in the United States, Esterline sent an OPIM cable to the Director requesting that Dick Drain, Chief of Operations, WH/4, attempt to contact Alejos to discuss the proposed secret agreement regarding the request by the government of Guatemala for US Special Forces trainers. But, unfortunately, Mr. Alejos, instead of being in Washington as anticipated, was somewhere in New York; and there was no possibility of getting his advice and guidance prior to the time that Esterline had his meeting with Ydigoras. 66/ In any event, the results of a two hour meeting that   and Esterline

---

* Alejos was coming to the United States at this time as a member of the Guatemalan coffee group -- thanks to the Agency's efforts on his behalf!

had with Ydigoras on the night of 14 December were
negative. The report of the meeting stated:

> Written agreement discussed in general
> terms, but not shown him [Ydigoras] as he
> said he would not sign any secret pact.
> Made reference to secret agreement he
> signed with Castillo Armas 1953 which has
> since caused him serious political prob-
> lems. Expressed continued willingness
> give any and all support, including re-
> ceiving training personnel, short of
> signing any agreement. 67/

The cable went on to request that Headquarters contact
Roberto Alejos requesting that he remain in Washington
to meet with Esterline and Robert Davis,
who would be flying up to Washington on 16 December --
the thought being that discussion with Alejos might yet
bring about a change in Ydigoras's thinking.

Esterline's remembrance of this visit to Ydigoras
is at some variance with both the cable traffic and subsequent events, but it is interesting to observe the comments which he did have to make on the subject:

> I actually, myself, executed with
> Ydigoras Fuentes the agreement. At the
> time that I did it -- in true name -- I
> thought "I suppose they'll be reading
> about this someday and I'll have to save
> that piece of paper." He [Ydigoras] said,
> "that piece of paper will never be exposed,"
> and it hasn't to my knowledge.

In response to a question of how it happened that he was sent to Guatemala, Esterline remarked:

> State said, "Oh, we don't want to touch that," and Ydigoras said, "well, I'm not going to do it unless it is signed by some responsible individual." We looked around the Agency and said to J. C. [King], "J. C., this kind of ..." "No, no," he said. "I don't think I ought to do that." He said, "Jake, you are in charge of the project, why don't you do it." So being a brash young man I said, "Well, we're never going to get this thing going unless somebody signs it."
>
> So I flew to Guatemala black with Roberto Alejos, who is now a substantial banker in Miami, and with Bob Davis, who [   ] [   ] at the time, and I think, with the powers and full knowledge of the Ambassador, although I didn't meet him because I was there black. I went in illegally and left illegally. We drew up the particulars of the base agreement -- if you will, a Status of Forces Agreement.

When asked if Bissell and Dulles were aware that he had been sent to negotiate with Ydigoras, Esterline's response was: "Oh, hell yes! Oh, hell yes! I went as an instructed delegate from Washington. The wording 'an expendable pawn.' No, I went on specific instruction from Bissell and Dulles.'" 68/*

---

* Despite Esterline's conviction that a piece of paper actually passed between himself and Ydigoras, the author thinks it more likely that Esterline's story, as noted above, reflects an honest confusion of the
(footnote continued on following page)

Esterline's failure to get Ydigoras to sign the Status of Forces Agreement must have gone down hard with Agency representatives because of the extreme difficulties that had been encountered in reaching an agreement with the Department of Defense, particularly the Army representatives, to undertake the negotiations in the first place. Richard D. Drain, who was Chief of Operations for the project at the time, in an oral interview with the author, told some other details of the story which are believed worth repeating here because Drain was involved in the negotiations with DOD and was responsible for drawing up the actual agreement which it was anticipated Ydigoras would sign. To the question of whether he had drawn up the agreement, Drain responded:

> Jesus, yes. On self-destructing paper. Well, this was all typical of the idiocy that prevailed because of the failure of Mr. Nixon to succeed Mr. Eisenhower. From the time the vote was in -- the first Tuesday after the first Monday in November -- up until JFK took the oath on January 20,

---

personnel and the details involved in the negotiations with the GOG at the time. As will be pointed out subsequently, what Esterline did sign was the agreement with Carlos Alejos, Guatemalan Ambassador to the United States.

the Eisenhower government was increasingly
zombie. You know, you would go over there
to talk to James Douglas Smith [sic], Undersecretary of Defense, and, "well, Mr. Smith
probably won't be in much any more, he is
in New York looking for a job. Mr. Irwin
is in charge," and so on.

I guess this is one of the maddest anybody ever saw Eisenhower because three
times the President of the United States
had to be involved in this weighty matter
-- should Special Forces troops be made
available to the Agency for this matter?
Doubly stupid because, as I said earlier,
Colonel Yarborough and Dick Drain were
entirely in accord on this. Yarborough
wanted these guys to get some Latin American
experience on the ground, and we desperately
needed them. Three times the cock crew before the President of the United States
had his order carried out. The first time
it was discussed the President of the United
States authorized it; and the Undersecretary
of Defense went back and told the Secretary
of the Army -- that goddamned fool Brucker,
or whatever his name was ... from Michigan
-- "You are authorized to do this."

I went over to see Yarborough, and expected to see him jump for joy; and he hadn't
gotten the message. So I take this problem
to Tracy Barnes and he says, "I think this
is something that we will negotiate." I
said, "Well, you do what you want with it,
but the President of the United States has
ordered it, and nothing is happening." He
said, "well, I will go see Jack Irwin."
Well, he came back with the word that the
President had not "directed" it, he had
only "authorized" it; and the Secretary
of the Army did not feel that "authorized"
to do something ... he was "required" to
do it. O.K., we take it back to the NSC,

and the President says, "Is that so ...
all right, I order it."   And, again,
nothing happened.

I checked with Yarborough, and it hasn't
dropped down his tube yet ... and find out
that the Secretary of the Army has said
that even though "directed," he has to, as
a statutory matter, assure that something
equal to the Status of Forces Agreement is
in effect with the host country, lest there
be a court martial proceeding ... or some
host country ... da, da, da ... and it goes
back to the President again. "Will you
authorize or direct that this be done, in
the absence of a special Status of Forces
Agreement," and the President of the United
States says ... "Goddamnit ... Blankety-
blank ... you do it!" So Mr. Barnes
"negotiated" it, and he came back saying
that if President Ydigoras will sign the
document that says that the Status of
Forces will apply -- even though not
technically in force -- then the Secretary
of the Army will let this go forward.

So, I worked with TSD to see if we could
come up with some paper which, after a
certain amount of time, whether exposed
to light or not, would just disintegrate.
Whether we actually typed it on such paper
or not, I don't know; but I wrote up a
very learned piece of paper, and goddamned
if Jake Esterline didn't have to drop everything else that he was doing and go down and
get the old Indian to sign this thing. 69/

In response to the query of the origin of the

idea for the Status of Forces Agreement, Drain explained

this as follows:

Well, now, I remember -- and I haven't
thought about it until this moment -- that

faced with this weighty problem which had
now lost us three weeks ... "directed" or
"authorized" ... I remember what Lucian K.
Truscott

70/*

How the actual negotiations in Washington were

conducted is not clear from the records that are now

available. In a Memorandum for the Director of Central

Intelligence dated 21 December 1960, however, C. Tracy

---

* During an Oral History (9 January 1976) interview,
Mr. Drain had indicated that Esterline had signed the
agreement with Ydigoras, but in a telecon with Mr.
Drain on 19 August 1976, when the author raised the
question of whether Drain was certain that Esterline
and Ydigoras had signed the agreement -- pointing out
to Drain the indications in the cable traffic were
contrary to this -- Drain said that he could not be
positive. With reference to the possibility of having
met with Roberto Alejos in Washington, Drain did remember one meeting that he had with Roberto Alejos and
his brother Carlos Alejos, the Ambassador to the United
States, in which he thought that this subject might
have been discussed and that Roberto Alejos did get
in touch with Ydigoras. Drain, however, could not be
positive that it had been over the matter of having
Carlos Alejos sign off on the Status of Forces Agreement. 70a/

Barnes, the A/DDP/A, mentioned among other things
"Although we failed to complete these arrangements
with Ydigoras [e.g., the signing of the Status of
Forces Agreement] we have since been successful in
making identical arrangements with the Guatemalan
Ambassador to Washington who acted as the Government
of Guatemala representative in place of Ydigoras." 71/
Esterline continued as the principal in the negotiations
that led to the signing of the agreement (21 December
1960) with the Guatemalan Ambassador.

This, however, was not the end of the story.
In a meeting on 22 December with representatives of
the Department of Defense, John M. Irwin, Assistant
Secretary for Defense and a newcomer to the negotiations, raised a question about the utility of the
secret agreement that had been signed; and he indicated that the agreement showing that the CIA was
providing US military forces to another government
to train personnel of that government would not serve
the primary purpose of providing a secure cover for
the SF trainers. As a result of Irwin's objections
it was decided that an attempt would be made to get

the Department of State to sign a Memorandum of Agreement with the Guatemalan Ambassador, setting forth that in response to a request from the Guatemalan government the US would provide military training for selected elements of the Guatemalan armed forces. 72/

The ball continued to bounce, however, with no one wanting to assume responsibility overtly for the United States Government action; and it was reported on 27 December 1960, for example, that in a meeting with Thomas Mann, the Assistant Secretary of State for American Republic Affairs, concerning the suggestion that State sign the agreement with the Guatemalan Ambassador:

> Mann was extremely hesitant to agree to any signature by a representative of the State Department to a document. After considerable discussion, however, he did agree to the possibility of having a Memorandum for the Record prepared (suggested draft attached) which could be signed by the Guatemalan Ambassador as an accurate statement of the understanding reached between the Government of Guatemala and the United States. The Department then could refer this signed memorandum to the Department of Defense for appropriate action. 73/

This, in fact, was the method that was finally evolved to solve the problem; and on 29 December 1960, Carlos

Alejos, Guatemalan Ambassador to the United States, signed the document.*

Once this document was completed -- and even before he had CIA's firm requirement in hand -- General Erskine, Assistant to the Secretary of Defense (Special Operations) -- issued instructions that active military personnel would be made available as requested by CIA. 73a/ In his formal request to the Office of Special Operations, on 5 January 1961, where he spelled out the detailed requirements for Special Forces personnel for the project, Jake Esterline neatly summarized the situation that had finally been resolved:

> Because DOD desired certain agreements
> between governments before it was willing
> to act affirmatively on the original [16
> November 1960] requirement, the Agency,
> with the approval and concurrence of the
> Department of State, negotiated an agree-
> ment with the host government which

---

* Appendix 2 contains copies of the complete set of documents involved in this episode of the Special Forces Trainers, and clearly illustrates the degree to which nits were picked on what to the pragmatist would appear to have been a relatively simple matter. Included in Appendix 2 are the four versions of the Memorandum of Agreement which Esterline initially attempted to negotiate with Ydigoras and the series of memos related to the Memorandum for Record which Ambassador Alejos eventually signed per the request of the Department of State.

provided protection for US military forces
in that country supporting project CROSS-
PATCH. A copy of this agreement was provided to DOD by memorandum dated 30 December 1960. 74/

H. The Changing Political Climate

Following resolution of the Special Forces program,

the beginning of the new year was marked by a spirit of

close cooperation between the Government of Guatemala

and the Agency's representatives.* Roberto Alejos, the

---

* The same could not be said for the degree of rapport
between the Department of State and the Government of
Guatemala. Between the end of November 1960 and the
beginning of 1961, there was a noticeable effort on
the part of the Department of State to keep US relations with Guatemala at something less than the level
of an *abrazo*. When planning a US response to President
Ydigoras's message thanking the US for instituting naval
operations which "prevented outside forces from giving
support to the Communist-inspired revolutionary movement,"
Secretary Herter cautioned the President that: "Since
the degree of direct involvement of pro-Communist and
pro-Castro elements in the recent Guatemalan uprising
has not yet been determined, the text of the suggested
reply reaffirms that our action was aimed at prevention
of intervention from abroad." 74a/

In planning a response to President Ydigoras's
greeting for the New Year, Secretary Herter again
cautioned: "The Department feels that an exchange
concerning the Cuban question with President Ydigoras
would not be appropriate at the present time. It is
recommended, therefore, that you merely acknowledge
briefly his telegram." 74b/ Even though this advice
was followed, the Department directed the Amembassy
Guatemala to understand that after delivering President Eisenhower's message: "White House desires text
this message not rpt not become public." 74c/

Minister of Defense of Guatemala, and the President
of Guatemala all visited the various training sites
and indicated considerable pleasure at the progress
that was being made. It was also reported that these
leaders of the GOG were impressed with both the trainees
and their armament; and considering the political un-
rest, it is possible that Ydigoras wanted to get some
idea of the materiel -- if not the personnel (Cuban)
-- that might be used for or against him in an emergency.
Where a few weeks earlier there had been some confusion
over airdrop operations training, by mid-January 1961
it was reported that there was close cooperation between [   ] and Roberto Alejos with regard to an upcoming
program of this nature.

To belay the charges that the GOG was permitting
CIA activities in his country, Roberto Alejos personally
escorted some *Time* magazine reporters and a photographer
and an NBC reporter whom President Ydigoras had invited
to visit the JMADD and TRAV sites. Prior to the reception of the newsmen, however, the Cuban trainees and
Agency personnel, except for several pilot instructors
and a couple of ground force trainers, had all been

moved either into restricted areas or out of sight of the newsmen -- the Cuban air trainees being orbited over the ocean in a C-54. Guatemalan soldiers were moved into the areas to pass as the ones who were being trained by the few Americans posing as mercenaries hired by the GOG to provide the training.

Ydigoras believed that the guided tour procedure was the best defense against both the heavy internal political pressures as well as the inquiries from out-side news sources for information on the activities which were being observed at the Retalhuleu airstrip. Through the device of admitting to a certain amount of US technical help in the form of "mercenaries" he hoped to blunt the charges that he was preparing and supporting the Cubans who planned to overthrow Castro. 75/*

US newspapers and periodicals began to show so much interest in possible CIA involvement in Guatemala

---

* Robert Zunzer, presently Executive Officer to the Deputy Director for Administration, clearly recalls having to take to the woods in order to get out of the path of the media investigators who were brought into Guatemala at this time. He said it provided one or two of the few days of leisure that he experienced during the course of his participation in the JMATE activity.

toward the end of 1960 that early in January 1971 Carlos Alejos, the Ambassador to the US, released a statement to the Associated Press from Guatemala's Minister of Defense, Colonel Enrique Peralta Azurdia, which claimed that all US military personnel in Guatemala were official members of the US Military Mission. The Minister of Defense not only stated that US personnel were engaged exclusively in training Guatemalan forces for self defense, but he went on to emphasize the GOG's fear of Castro and communist intervention:

> Guatemala is not an aggressor country, Guatemala is not receiving ten ships every week loaded with war material [*sic*] and equipment manufactured in Communist countries. Guatemala has no Chinese Communist instructors. Guatemala has no jet Communist planes. Guatemala has no Communist guided rockets and missiles. The only thing Guatemala has is men with great hearts ready to fight for their independence and political liberties. Batista is not in Guatemala, but Arbenz is in Cuba. 75a/

Even more significant was that the news stories inspired some members of the US Congress to make inquiries about CIA involvement; and this, in turn, caused President Eisenhower to express himself very strongly on the constitutional issue of the separation of powers. In a 10 January 1961 meeting of the Special Group, the

President reportedly:

> Raised certain questions as to the
> right of a [Congressional] committee to
> ask questions on foreign policy affecting
> the security of the United States. He
> commented that when this is demanded as a
> right you are "sunk," and wondered how
> much right have they got, inasmuch as the
> Constitution says that it is the responsi-
> bility of the Chief Executive. 75b/*

In an attempt to divert attention from the Agency,
Chief, WHD apparently forwarded a suggestion that the
Agency sponsored Cuban exile organization, the FRD,
publicly acknowledge that it was involved in sponsor-
ing the military training in Guatemala. Jake Esterline,
however, noted that such an admission would contradict
statements already issued by the Government of Guatemala; and he also emphasized that it would be used by

---

* It is assumed that this was a Special Group meeting.
In addition to the President, the attendees were the
usual members of the Special Group on Cuba -- National
Security Adviser Gordon Gray, Secretary of Defense
Gates, Deputy Secretary of Defense Douglas, Under
Secretary of State Merchant, Assistant Secretary of
State Mann, and Ambassador Whiting Willauer. (Wil-
lauer was Eisenhower's appointee to assist the incoming
Kennedy Administration in the transfer of the anti-
Castro activities.) The memorandum of the meeting,
however, was prepared by Colonel J. C. King, Chief,
WH Division, not by Thomas A. Parrott who normally
acted as Secretary for Special Group sessions. 75c/

the opponents of Ydigoras to discredit his administration. 75d/ Initially, however, Col. King must have ignored Esterline's warning; but the DCI failed to support King's Plan. 75e/

The hassle with the media would continue throughout the course of the Bay of Pigs operation, but in no instance did the Government of Guatemala back off from providing cover for the training activity being sponsored by the Agency at Guatemalan sites. If anything, the GOG went to extremes to protect the cover story. In late March 1961, for example, following an article in the *Washington Post* which stated "an army estimated at several thousands is presently training at a clandestine camp in Guatemala," Carlos Urrutia-Aparaicio, Guatemala's Ambassador to the OAS, wrote a letter to the editor of the *Post* stating:

> On behalf of my government I categorically deny this to be a fact. Not one Cuban exile is receiving training in Guatemala. There are several hundred of them in my country, but we strictly enforce the Pan American instruments governing territorial asylum. Whenever these have been overlooked or disregarded, my government has immediately requested the Cuban refugees concerned to leave the country.
>
> It is our own army which is getting military training, but for defensive

reasons alone. The present democratic and constitutional government of Guatemala is duty-bound to defend itself from extracontinental forces based on Cuba, which are determined to overthrow it by force. Nobody can deny Guatemala the immemorial right to self-defense, recognized as such by the Charter of the Organization of American States and the Charter of the United Nations. 76/

The training facilities in Guatemala also had other visitors during the early part of 1961 -- the leaders of the FRD, Tony Varona, Antonio Maceo, and Manuel Artime. The FRD visit was precipitated in large part because of charges that were filtering back to Miami that the Batistiano factions were trying to penetrate -- or perhaps had even captured -- the leadership in the training camps at JMTRAV and JMADD. In mid-February 1961, the FRD leaders were moved to Guatemala by black flight; and they were met by Roberto Alejos, who played host for a session at which Ydigoras was in attendance. Prior to the meeting Ydigoras had indicated to [   ] and to Jake Esterline who was in Guatemala, that "he [Ydigoras] will handle meeting any way Agency desires, i.e., stressing need for Cuban unity, need to keep military leadership apolitical based on ability, etc." 77/

With the reorganization of the political structure of the Cuban exile group in the United States demanded by the Kennedy administration, the leaders of the newly formed Cuban Revolutionary Council (CRC) visited Guatemala from 29-31 March 1961. Again Roberto Alejos played host and President Miguel Ydigoras Fuentes met with Jose Miro Cardona, Chairman of the CRC, Tony Varona, Manuel Artime, and Carlos Hevia. Once again Ydigoras lectured the Cuban political leaders about the need for unity and cooperation with the US government, and once again the political leaders were impressed by the visit to the training facilities at JMTRAV and JMADD. 78/*

I. Third Country Involvement

During the summer of 1960, as negotiations were proceeding with Guatemala for the training bases, an incident occurred which foreshadowed one of the few areas where the US would be in contention with the GOG during the course of Project JMATE. In a cable of

_____

* This visit of the CRC leaders to Guatemala in March of 1961 caused considerable consternation to President Somoza of Nicaragua when he learned that his country would not be visited by the CRC.

10 July, Guatemala informed the Director that British
military maneuvers were being planned for Belize
(British Honduras); and Ydigoras had informed [ ]
[   ] that the GOG would have to send troops and
planes to the border in order to maintain the prestige
of his country if the maneuvers were held. GOG requested
that [   ] try to get Washington to intervene with the
British to call off the exercise. 78a/* Whatever
action was taken, the JMATE project personnel were
not concerned with the Belize issue again until 14 February 1961 when Ydigoras requested that Chief, JMATE
and [ ] meet with him to discuss the subject.

He gave [   ] and Chief, JMATE the
original of a paper on Belize which "he requested be
given to appropriate authorities within the Department
of State" -- a rather interesting method for transmitting material to the Department when the US had an
Ambassador in Guatemala City! Ydigoras emphasized that

---

* Whether the Agency actually approached State at this
time has not been investigated for purposes of this history. There is no question, however, that the Department was well aware of the dispute between the GOG and
Britain over Belize.

his government had been negotiating for some time
with Her Majesty's Government over the subject of
granting greater autonomy to the Government of Belize
on economic matters, particularly on the right of that
colony to negotiate reciprocal trade agreements with
its neighbors. As pointed out to the Agency's representatives by Jesus Unda Marillo, the Guatemalan
Foreign Minister, Jorge Garcia Granades, Guatemala's
Special Representative on Belize affairs, and Ian Munn,
the son-in-law of Ydigoras, the economic development
program which the GOG was then promoting for the Petén
area, bordering Belize, was dependent in considerable
degree upon reciprocal trade relations with that
British colony. Although not specified in the discussions, Chief, JMATE believed that what the Government of Guatemala wanted specifically was a guarantee
of a direct outlet to the sea for the oil, chicle,
timber and other products from Petén.

Both Chief, JMATE and   told Ydigoras
that international negotiations such as had been discussed were not within the province of the Agency, but
they did agree to give the paper to State:

> The President and the Foreign Minister
> both indicated their desire that said
> paper come to the attention of Mr. Adolph
> [*sic*] Berle, a man whose past career
> they seemed to know very well. C/JMATE
> assured them that this would be done. 79/

Available records do not indicate that the Agency was further involved in the promotion of this particular activity on the part of the GOG, however, it was quite clear that Ydigoras continued to be very sensitive about Belize.

In March of 1961, one of the JMADD C-54's was forced to land in Jamaica after an airdrop over Cuba -- said aircraft having filed a flight plan out of San Jose, Guatemala. Unfortunately, the GOG had not given prior authorization for this flight plan. When word from Jamaica apparently got out that the flight originated at San Jose, Roberto Alejos was constrained to make an immediate press release denying that the aircraft had ever come out of Guatemala, and he suggested that the British were tyring to embarrass the Guatemalan Government, in part, at least, so that there would be no pressure for negotiations on the Belize issue. In any event, Headquarters sent an OPIM cable to Guatemala recommending that Alejos and Ydigoras

be dissuaded from making any press release which
would be critical of the British for it was pointed
out to [ ] that the British had been most
helpful in terms of getting the C-54 released and in
cancelling the original flight plan without any further
publicity. 80/*

J. GOG - JMATE and the Kennedy Administration

Even though President Ydigoras had already assured
the Agency that the training activity could continue,
he felt some concern about the change of administrations
in the US; and an EMERGENCY cable from [ ]
on 25 February 1961 indicated that [ ] had been called
to a meeting with Ydigoras. [ ] was told that Ydigoras
was writing a personal letter to President Kennedy

---

* At the end of 1961, in his New Year's Eve speech
of 31 December 1961, Ydigoras for the first time acknowledged that his government had participated with
the exiled Cuban leaders, and that Guatemala had been
used as a training site for the Bay of Pigs invasion.
In that same speech he reportedly said that as a fair
price the "friendly government" that was supporting
the Cuban exiles -- the US -- had agreed "to request
good offices to convince Britain to return Belize to
us under certain conditions, acceptable to a majority
of that colony's inhabitants." Reportedly the training activity did not begin until after this agreement
with the US had been reached. 80a/

setting forth his views and recommendations on policy vis-a-vis Cuba, particularly suggesting that it was time to get the Cuban Brigade off the dime and into action. The letter was to be hand carried to JFK by Roberto Alejos, and ⬚⬚⬚⬚⬚⬚⬚ was to accompany Alejos to Washington.

During a private luncheon with Ydigoras and Alejos, ⬚⬚⬚⬚⬚⬚⬚ heard the discussion of the proposed letter that was being readied for President Kennedy. Among other things, the letter would point out that Ydigoras, more than any other Latin American leader, was taking direct action to oppose the spread of Castro communism and cited the 13 November 1960 revolt as a part of that plot -- though as has been noted, there was no evidence of Cuban involvement. Ydigoras pointed out that it was his firm conviction that the Brigade -- both air force and infantry -- was quite ready; and remarking on the Cuban temperament suggested that if they weren't engaged soon they were very likely to lose their spirit and be unwilling to continue. Moreover, the Guatemalan President emphasized that the longer the Brigade delayed its invasion, the more training the Castro militia was going to have and the more difficult it would be for the Brigade to overcome them.

Ydigoras claimed that there was extensive anti-Castro sentiment throughout Cuba and that if the attack took place soon, this force could be applied in support of the invasion. Continuing he noted that since Kennedy had said that he was opposed to Castro, the United States should actively support the anti-Castro move-ment at this time. By so doing, the standing of the US in the eyes of Latin America would be greatly enhanced and Kennedy would be looked on as a savior who kept his promises. Ydigoras closed the letter by saying that if the attack were postponed much longer, the people of Cuba would lose faith that anything could be done, the insurrectionists in the Escambray would be defeated, and other governments in Latin America would be even more fearful and subject to takeover by the leftists.

Copies of this letter dated 28 February apparently hit the Department of State like a lead balloon. In a chance meeting with Ydigoras,   was told that after a session with Thomas Mann the Guatemalan Ambassador, Carlos Alejos, felt that the Guatemalan cause was lost. [   ] apparently was unaware of the contents of the Ydigoras letter to Kennedy which presumably precipitated Mann's reaction, but in any event, he cabled OPIM to Headquarters reporting on Ydigoras's feeling.

Roberto Alejos was successful in setting up a meeting with President Kennedy on 7 March 1961 -- with Thomas Mann and an Agency representative also in attendance.* The letter from the President of Guatemala, which incidentally had been prepared in both Spanish and in a bad English translation, was discussed.** Mann's Memorandum of Conversation and copies of the Spanish and English versions of Ydigoras's letter were transmitted to Ralph Dungan of the White House Staff on 16 March 1961, and in the transmittal it was noted

----

* It is believed that Tracy Barnes, rather than Jake Esterline, represented the Agency.

** The English translation had been prepared by GOG not by State.

that the material had been reviewed by the Secretary
of State. In the transmittal to Dungan, the Department said:

> As you will note, President Ydigoras'
> letter takes up extremely sensitive
> matters regarding Cuba. We believe that
> the President's comments on March 7 to
> Mr. Alejos obviate the need for any writ-
> ten reply to President Ydigoras. More-
> over, it is believed that it would not
> be desirable in any case to reply in
> writing to the letter. 81/*

---

* Of interest with reference to the letter from Ydigoras
to President Kennedy are the following: In briefing
the Special Group on 2 March 1961, the DCI noted:

> That [Roberto] Alejos is in Washington with
> a letter from President Ydigoras addressed
> to President Kennedy, and that he is attempt-
> ing through his brother, the Guatemalan Am-
> bassador [Carlos Alejos], to obtain an appoint-
> ment with Mr. Kennedy. Mr. Dulles said that
> he understood the letter took a strong posi-
> tion on the necessity of early action, vis-
> a-vis Cuba, but -- in answer to a question --
> assured the group that we [CIA] had neither
> written nor inspired the letter. 82/

Then, whether incidental or intentional, at that
same meeting, "Mr. Dulles also said that he thought we
should discuss soon with the Special Group actions to
be taken with respect to employment of the forces now
in training in Guatemala." In other words, the identical subject that Ydigoras was raising with President
Kennedy.

In 1964, when he appeared in an NBC television
White Paper on the Bay of Pigs, Roberto Alejos put a
somewhat different emphasis on the meeting that was

(footnote continued on following page)

Shortly, following the visit of Roberto Alejos
to the Department of State, Carlos Alejos, the Ambassador of Guatemala to the United States, paid a formal
call on Secretary of State Rusk "mainly to get acquainted
and to extend greetings personally and in behalf of President Ydigoras." Wymberley Coerr, the Deputy Assistant
Secretary for American Republic Affairs, who would replace Thomas Mann, and Richard Godfrey, the Officer in
charge of Guatemalan affairs, were also in attendance
at this session, along with an interpreter. The Department of State Memorandum of Conversation is couched in
the general platitudes of diplomatic language and while
Alejos probably was hoping to get some support from the
Department for the employment of the Cuban Brigade against
Castro, nonesuch was forthcoming. What he got instead
was the "big picture" about developments of an inter-
American, anti-Castro program from Secretary Rusk.
One interesting comment which appeared in State's

---

held with Kennedy. He said that he came to Washington
at the request of President Ydigoras to discuss getting
the Brigade out of Guatemala. 83/ Although this was
of concern to Ydigoras, this was not the principal
thrust of the letter which Alejos carried to Kennedy.
Ydigoras's principal concern was whether the Brigade
was in fact going to be employed in an attempt to oust
Fidel Castro from Cuba.

memorandum -- particularly in view of the position
later adopted by the Secretary of State -- was the
following:

> The Secretary said the United States
> was concerned because a number of Latin
> American countries did not see the threat
> from Communism as clearly as did the
> Foreign Minister or else these countries
> felt certain restraints in dealing with
> it. 84/

In early April 1961, Jake Esterline had a session
at State to give Adolf A. Berle a thorough briefing on
the recently completed visit of the CRC leaders to
Guatemala and to give Berle some positive guidance
for his upcoming visit with Jose Miro Cardona.* Chief,
WH/4 also discussed the planned operation, particularly
the negative effects that a cancellation of the projected
strike against Cuba would have on US relations not only
with the Government of Guatemala, but also on the whole
of Latin America -- particularly those nations with
ambivalent feelings about Communism. Esterline

---

* Esterline mentioned that, among other topics, Dr.
Miro probably would raise questions about US funds for
a new Cuban government, US recognition and open support,
use of US personnel with the Cuban Brigade at the time
of the invasion, and US reaction to various Cuban political leaders.

"concluded his remarks by saying that the cancellation
blow would be so severe that the administration's
plans for the Western Hemisphere, which have received
so much publicity, would probably lose all meaning." 85/

During the period immediately prior to the invasion, but after the bulk of the Cuban forces and
the operational aircraft from JMADD had departed Guatemala, President Ydigoras requested that he receive
daily situation reports in case he had to respond to
either internal or foreign crises which might result
because of GOG support for the Brigade. In the confusion attendant upon the operation, the system could
not be maintained; and on 19 April 1961, following
attacks on the GOG in the United Nations and by the
opposition Congressmen in Guatemala, Ydigoras informed
[   ] that he had been forced to agree to permit a visit
to Retalhuleu and to the La Suiza site by opposition
Congressmen. JMADD was ordered to sterilize the base
in the same manner as had been done three months earlier
when the newsmen had been escorted through the area.
Two US "mercenaries" were to remain on the base as
advisers and all the other Agency personnel, including

communicators, and Cubans were ordered to go to TRAV.
The Agency was to provide two bilingual advisers to
be in attendance at La Suiza when the Congressmen came
through on their inspection. Moreover, a halt was
called on all incoming flights to JMADD until further
notice. 86/

That Ydigoras was expecting some domestic difficulties was apparent in a cable from [   ] to Headquarters
reading: "GOG request and [   ] concurs immediate air-
shipment 500 to 1,000 tear gas grenades for use control
possible mob activities next few days." This went forward to Headquarters on 19 April 1961, 87/*

The Agency also displayed considerable concern
for its commitment to the Ydigoras government in the
period following the collapse of the invasion; and
early in May, in response to Ydigoras's request that
the Agency continue to support the training activity
for a Guatemalan Special Battalion until the end of

----

* In anticipation of possible difficulties from his
political opposition, Ydigoras had requested that [   ]
make inquiries about the possibility of obtaining a
100-man pack for caching. It is not known, however,
if these weapons were obtained, even though a number
of such packs reached Florida between 17 March 1961
and 17 April 1961. 88/

June -- JMATE already had made a commitment to support it through May -- [   ] supported the request. He made the case that this was a security measure because the press was still trying to prove that the Cuban Brigade had training bases in Guatemala. [   ] furthermore noted that continuing the training of the Guatemalan Battalion would help to deter the revolutionary activities against the Ydigoras Government. 89/

Headquarters approved the request for the additional support, but one problem did come up -- the question of whether or not the Special Forces trainers would be continued through the month of June. The Special Forces personnel began to get quite edgy because their commitment had only been through the end of May, and [   ] was notified that if the training of the Guatemalan Battalion was completed by 20 May, the Special Forces personnel would then be returned. Pushing for an earlier exit, the Special Forces personnel had contended that the Guatemalan trainees and officers were completely indifferent toward the ongoing training activity. Headquarters did say that while the SF trainers would be released

beginning on 20 May, [   ] was not to approve
any departures of Special Forces personnel until further
authorization from Headquarters. 90/

How close the ties between the Government of
Guatemala and the Agency's representatives were was
revealed late in April 1961 at a meeting that was
called at the request of Carlos Alejos, the Ambassador
to the United States from Guatemala. He requested that
Jake Esterline meet with him at the embassy residence
to discuss some sensitive information that he had
recently received from his brother, Roberto. The
sensitive information concerned an offer that General
Trujillo of the Dominican Republic had reportedly made
to both President Ydigoras and to President Somoza of
Nicaragua to make available to them, in the Dominican
Republic, airfields, training sites, and other facilities needed to continue to wage war against Castro.
According to the report that Esterline prepared on the
meeting "the only *quid pro quo* involved would be that
the United States give sanction to this arrangement
in the first instance and, in the second instance,
agree to let Trujillo live out the rest of his days

in peace without further interference from the United States." Carlos Alejos said further that his brother, Roberto, had been authorized by President Ydigoras to deal with Somoza and Trujillo on the matter; and what Roberto Alejos was looking fôr, because of this responsibility, was some reaction from the US, directing his attention not to the US Department of State but to the Central Intelligence Agency.

Chief, WH/4 apparently suggested that there was some problem in dealing with Trujillo because of his "unsavory" reputation; and this suggestion was not particularly well received by Ambassador Alejos, who,

> with some heat replied that Trujillo may
> be unpopular, but he is certainly anti-
> Communist and prepared to do something,
> whereas the alleged great friends of the
> United States, such as Figueres of Costa
> Rica and President Betancourt of Venezuela,
> have made many friendly noises but never
> once have made a firm offer of real estate
> or material [sic] support to the battle
> against Castro.

The Ambassador went on to indicate that since the collapse of the invasion he had been getting what he considered a rather unfavorable reaction from Adolf Berle and other members of the State Department with whom he had been holding discussions. This, perhaps,

explains why he had come to the Agency with this particular story rather than going to the Department. In

any event, however, Chief, WH/4 ended his memorandum

with the following suggestions:

> Action required: Exposure of the Trujillo
> offer to the DDP and or other interested
> parties and early advice to the Guatemalan
> Ambassador with simultaneous notification
> to [   ] of the
> answer given.
>
> Recommendation: That acceptance of assist-
> ance from Trujillo be given the greatest
> scrutiny. In the writer's judgment, ex-
> posure of Trujillo's assistance at this
> time could well swing increasing support
> to the United States in the wrong direc-
> tion. No serious consideration should,
> therefore, be given to this offer. 91/

Except for the story of the retrograde and dis-
position of the materiel which will be discussed in

a later volume, this concludes the story of the Agency's

policy related -- if not policy making -- contacts with

the Government of Guatemala during the course of

Project JMATE. Agency representatives rather than

Department of State personnel dealt directly with the

President of Guatemala and his closest associates over

actions which involved relationships with the United

States Government and bore heavily on the formulation

of US policy for Guatemala. There is little question

that in his choice of working with the Agency rather

than with the US Ambassador in Guatemala, John J.

Muccio, Ydigoras was no fool. As [   ], who [   ]

[   ] on 1 December 1960 indicated,

relations between [   ] and the Ambassador were

strained to the point where the [   ] "operated al-

most as a separate entity until the departure of the

Ambassador in the Fall of 1961." 92/*

If the oral history interview which Muccio made

for the John F. Kennedy Library in the Spring of 1971

is indicative of his character, it is understandable

why relations between Muccio and Agency personnel were

strained. In that interview, the pertinent portions

of which are reproduced in Appendix 3, Muccio tried to

indicate on the one hand that he was uninformed about

CIA activities in Guatemala, yet on the other hand he

---

* As indicated earlier in this chapter, [   ] and
[   ] overlapped as [   ]
[   ] and, in fact, each [
in his own particular bailiwick -- [   ] with the
Bay of Pigs Operation, and [   ] with the operation
[   ]. Muccio's successor, John Bell,
was named 10 November 1961. 93/

pointed to an unidentified Agency contact who was
keeping him fully posted on the Agency's operations.
As revealed in the cable traffic, Muccio participated
in various of the operations related to Project JMATE
-- both before and after the fact. Some of Muccio's
remarks in the JFK Library interview may have been
the reflection of interviewer biases, but they also
indicated that Muccio was trying to avoid any tie-in
with the "bad guys" of CIA.*

---

* The question of interviewer bias, for example, shows
through in the following comment made at one point:
"The whole ineptitude of the [Bay of Pigs] operation
is amazing, not only what you [Muccio] are talking
about now, but I was struck by the simple tactics at
the beach. It was just incredible to me that it could
have been done that way, but that's an aside, my opinion."
With this kind of "an aside" could the interviewee not
have detected a bias of the interviewer?

During the course of the operation
[of the air base at Puerto Cabezas] I
had one security officer ... He came
up to me quite concerned ... He said,
"We've got a bunch of Nicaraguans who
are ... in our secure area ... What'll
I do?" ... I looked out ... Christ Al-
mighty! ... They were all generals and
were led by [General] Somoza ... I said,
"It's their country, you had better let
them come in." So they came in and we
gave them a general briefing ... But
Somoza was concerned ... His concern
was the United States willingness to
follow through.

Garfield M. Thorsrud
to
Jack B. Pfeiffer
6 February 1976

Part II

Nicaragua

A. Background

Although Project JMATE operations in Nicaragua were of considerably shorter duration than in Guatemala, there were many similarities in the degree to which CIA personnel were involved directly with the nation's President or his close personal staff on issues which were of direct importance to US foreign policy. This section therefore, focuses on the relations between the Agency and President Luis Somoza Debayle. The internal situation in Nicaragua presented the Department of State with difficult choices. Somoza was an absolute dictator and, particularly after the 1960 election of John F. Kennedy, State was much concerned that, in appearance at least, the *abrazo* for Somoza be formal rather than friendly, lest the US risk loss of support in the OAS and UN from the reputedly "democratic" Central and South American nations. The Agency had no such problems -- it needed a base from which to mount air operations against Castro's Cuba; and the most likely available site outside CONUS was in Nicaragua.

B. Initiation of Discussions with President Somoza

Puerto Cabezas on the northeastern coast of Nicaragua lies approximately 650 miles due south of Havana. During WWII, Puerto Cabezas had been developed as one of the principal airfields in that country; and despite having fallen into some disrepair, it nonetheless looked like the most feasible site for launching air activities against Castro.* On 13 June 1960, less than three months following Eisenhower's decision to act against Castro, [   ]

[   ] Louis P. Napoli, had made arrangements to talk privately with President Somoza about Central American politics with particular emphasis on Cuban activities in the area. At this first meeting, President Somoza made it quite clear that he needed assurances that the United States Government would back whatever actions or operations were to be put in motion to the end of overthrowing Castro. 1/

---

* On 10 December 1960, the Puerto Cabezas facility was assigned the crypt JMTIDE.

Although he was [   ] [   ] in July of 1960, Lou Napoli was sent TDY to Managua to participate in a meeting between Agency representatives and the President of Nicaragua in September 1960. Accompanied by [   ] Walter S. Holloway, the CIA representatives met with President Somoza on 17 and 19 September 1960. 2/ The purpose of Napoli's TDY was to inform Somoza that the Frente Revolucionario Democrático (FRD) was the organ- ization of anti-Castro Cuban exiles which deserved the support of Somoza's government. This information for Somoza was in response to a question he had raised with Napoli in the previously mentioned June meeting. 3/

Somoza agreed that he would receive an FRD repre- sentative to discuss the situation and in addition indi- cated that he would make available a landing strip at Puerto Cabezas, a training site for about 100 men, and a shortwave radio station.* The Nicaraguan leader was not at all reluctant to raise pointed questions with

---

* The radio station, incidentally, that had been used during the course of operation PBSUCCESS which resulted in the ouster of the leftist Arbenz government in Guat- emala in 1958.

the CIA representatives, asking specifically what the position of the United States Government would be toward his country if Cuba should formally charge -- in the OAS or the UN -- that Nicaragua was fomenting war against them. Somoza wanted it understood and accepted by all levels of the US government that Nicaragua was on the side of the angels and, therefore, no US official should be allowed to attack Nicaragua for either its actions or its position vis-a-vis Cuba. Depite his cordial relations with the United States Ambassador, Thomas E. Whelan, Napoli reported that Somoza believed that:

> There are some long-haired, Department of State liberals who are not in favor of Somoza and they would welcome the chance to use this as a source of embarrassment to his government by verbally blasting his country for her actions against Cuba. 4/

It should be emphasized, however, that in dealing with the Nicaraguan leaders, the Agency representatives, while expressing that in their own opinions Somoza's requests were reasonable, did make clear that they spoke only for themselves. Their views did not represent formal US policy -- that would have to come from higher levels. 5/ Napoli was quite specific in saying that:

It is the opinion of the writer that
guidance must be passed to Holloway by
Headquarters in line with Somoza's query
in order that [   ] will be properly
informed and prepared to answer Somoza's
questioning on this matter. This query
is certain to arise again from time to
time until a satisfactory reply is given
to Somoza. 6/*

Napoli also indicated that:

The Acting Chief of the US Embassy
further said that inasmuch as he had no
instructions or prior notice of the mission,
plus the fact that only the US Ambassador
to Nicaragua was authorized to sit in
talks, he would prefer to remain clear of

---

* The Department of State representatives in the
foreign areas which were the sites of JMATE operations
frequently got quite goosey, particularly those of less
than ambassadorial ranks. In this instance, for example, [   ] noted in his transmittal:

The aspect of urgency which brought
Napoli to Managua has given the Acting
Chief of the American Embassy the impression that we might be operating on a non-
coordinated, uncontrolled, free wheeling
basis ... particularly since Napoli was
[   ]. [   ] has
done much to overcome past administrative
resistance here and improve the relationship of this office with the rest of State,
the cooperation of which we need. It is
incumbent upon the Agency that the American
Ambassador be thoroughly briefed while he
is in the United States on the circumstances
of Napoli's visit to insure no future con-
flict of interests and continued maintenance of rapport. 7/

any talks that Napoli had with Somoza.
This was agreeable to Napoli. The writer
wishes to emphasize that relations between Napoli and the Acting Chief of the
American Embassy remain completely cordial
and no change is anticipated. 8/

In mid-October of 1960, a survey team from Agency

Headquarters under the direction of Napoli made a trip

to Nicaragua to inspect Puerto Cabezas. Again the

Agency representatives dealt directly with the Presi-

dent of this Central American country, receiving his

full support and cooperation. Somoza volunteered to

foot the cost of the DC-3 aircraft that would be pro-

vided to the survey team, including the pilot and the

crew. He also was asked to provide a senior official

who could act as his spokesman, and in this connection

Noel Pallais Debayle, a cousin of Somoza's who had

accompanied the survey team, was identified as the

contact. Except for Napoli, who [   ]

[   ], the other members of the

survey team travelled as [   ] looking for

opportunities in Nicaragua.* The visit by the Agency

---

* The other members of the survey team included E. A.
Stanulis, who was Executive Officer for WH/4, Ralph
Brown, a logistics officer, Norman Imler and Robert
Moore, PM officers.

- 105 -

representatives had been cleared by Napoli with the
US Ambassador to Nicaragua, Thomas Whelan; and, in
addition, WH/4 had advised Frank Devine of the Department of State of the trip and Col. King had informed
Thomas Mann. 9/*

In a meeting with the leader of the survey team
(Napoli) on 14 Oct 60, Somoza agreed, among other things,
that the airstrip area could be isolated for the exclu-
sive use of the Agency. Somoza would provide a guard
force, construction of some temporary housing for personnel at the base would be permitted, and initially
he would help out with the transportation and supplies
for repairing the airstrip. He agreed to the use of
a practice bombing range on a nearby lagoon about 10
miles south of Puerto Cabezas; he agreed to the use
of Puerto Cabezas as a strike base for attacks on Cuba;
and he also agreed to permit the exile air force to
use the Nicaraguan Air Force insignia during any internal flights. It also was apparent that at least

------

* Mr. Mann was Assistant Secertary of State for Inter-
American Affairs and Mr. Devine was Special Assistant
to Mr. Mann.

two US companies located in the Puerto Cabezas area
would play significant roles in the Agency's plans for
Puerto Cabezas. Facilities of the Nicaraguan Long
Leaf Pine Company (NIPCO), a lumber company controlling
the terminal facilities, and the Standard Fruit Company,
controlling the rail line and the docking facility,
were critical to both planned air and maritime operations. 10/

In return for his support, Somoza wanted assurance
that once action against Castro started, there would
be no backing down by the USG; and he also wanted to
be sure that the proper levels of the US Government
were sanctioning the activities of the survey team.
When he was told that the US Ambassador was thoroughly
familiar with and involved in the planning, he was
somewhat mollified; but he did raise the question of
wanting a contact to whom he could turn if he believed
that the operation was not going as it should -- or
if he had complaints or suggestions to offer. Somoza
was told in this connection that the best thing he
could do would be to go to Holloway. As before, Napoli
made clear that these talks were exploratory and that

they represented no firm commitment. Somoza, of course, was told that he was dealing with [   ]; but there is little doubt that he knew exactly with whom he was negotiating.

Following the return of the survey team toward the end of October 1960, representatives from WH/4/PM, WH/4/Support, and DPD recommended that:

    1. Policy approval be obtained for the use of the Puerto Cabezas complex.

    2. Repair of the airstrip be commenced at once for JMARC use and as a long term CIA asset because of its overall strategic location.

    3. Construction of buildings be commenced for an air-maritime base, including storage of ordnance, ZRMEDRICK pack, and other supplies.

    4. An infantry training/holding base be constructed if no facility is to be made available in the US. 11/*

C. Rip Robertson's Excursion into Diplomacy

Following the return of the survey team in October, Napoli was succeeded by William "Rip" Robertson

---

* As a portent of things to come, the team recommended that it would be advisable to acquire the infantry base because of the crowded conditions at the Guatemala base.

as the Agency's principal contact with President Somoza.
In August of 1960 Robertson wrote to the Agency from
Nicaragua indicating that a business venture in which
he had been involved was terminating. A former contract
employee, he asked if there was any need for his services
at this time. His letter went forward from
to the DDCI, General Cabell; and it ended up with the
Deputy Director for Plans who suggested to Chief, WH
Division (Col. J. C. King) that Robertson be brought
into the JMARC program for operations in Nicaragua. 12/

With the concurrence of Chief, WH/4, Jake Esterline, Col. King prepared a Letter of Instruction (LOI)
for Robertson on 2 December 1960. The LOI confirmed
Robertson's verbal orders to proceed to Nicaragua as
coordinator of JMATE activities in that area. Among
other of the operational duties and responsibilities
Robertson was told:

> You will have authority over all JMARC
> personnel and responsibility for the coor-
> dination of all JMARC activities, including
> JMTIDE, as set forth in Para 11. You will
> be the sole JMARC official in contact with
> the President of Nicaragua and authorized
> to be in Nicaragua. 13/

Although cautioned concerning the responsibilities
of the US Ambassador in Nicaragua and the relationship

of [   ] to the Ambassador, Robertson was given a free hand to determine the extent of his contact with other US personnel in the Managua area. As a point of some contention, Robertson was also told that he would "be responsible for the coordination and general supervision of JMTIDE construction activities and air and maritime operational activities, when implemented under their specialized senior officers". 14/

Rip's Letter of Instruction indicated that the facility at JMTIDE should be completed by 15 January 1961, and that as soon as Robertson concluded satisfactory arrangements with the President of Nicaragua, the 5-man construction team would be sent black into the Puerto Cabezas area to conduct a survey estimating the scope and cost of the work. And then, somewhat paradoxically, in view of the previous comment about Robertson's authority, it was stated that:

> On Headquarter's approval of the plan
> for base construction, a Base Manager will
> be provided, with the responsibility for
> maintenance, operation and support of the
> facility. On activation, JMARC/PM Personnel
> will be assigned in connection with both
> air and maritime operations, and your
> responsibilities regarding these various
> JMTIDE activities include:

1. Being the sole JMARC channel to the President and Government of Nicaragua;

2. Assisting and expediting local procurement of materials and equipment; and

3. Assuring that JMARC security and general operating standards are maintained at JMTIDE. 15/

Even though the matter of the base at Puerto Cabezas had not yet been formally resolved, it was apparent, as Robertson was getting ready to depart for Headquarters, that the air element in DPD which had been assigned to the JMATE function was readying itself to move into action at the base. Not only were plans outlined for the survey team to go to Nicaragua at the earliest opportunity following Robertson's negotiations, but plans for housing, messing, cover, security, and air operations also were being outlined by Jim Cunningham, Assistant Chief/DPD, before the end of November. 16/*

Robertson's assignment in Nicaragua, which had been preceded by Napoli's trip in mid-October 1960,

---

* At this time operations anticipated maximum sortie rates of 100 a month for 3 months and probable maximum numbers of aircraft to be accommodated as 10 B-26's, 4 C-46's and at least two C-54's.

caused varying reactions within the Department of
State. U. S. Ambassador, Thomas Whelan, was a strong
supporter of the Somoza government; and, consequently,
looked with great favor on the Agency's attempts to
negotiate directly with Somoza, believing that this
was a proper step, not only from the US point of view
vis-a-vis Cuba, but also in terms of our relations
with the government of Nicaragua. 17/ On the other
hand, Thomas Mann, 18/ the Assistant Secretary of
State for Inter American Affairs, preferred to tread
very cautiously with regard to Nicaragua, adhering
to the formalities of diplomatic nicety vis-a-vis that
government. Within the Agency itself, Mr. Bissell's
Assistant Deputy Director of Plans for Action (ADDP/A),
C. Tracy Barnes, was apparently nervous about the
implications of using the Nicaraguan site because
Somoza was such a bad guy; and Barnes at one point
stated that "in the long run, we would lose an unacceptable amount of face with these [more democratic?]
countries" in Central America if we worked closely
with Somoza. 19/ Barnes, however, did realize the
urgent need for developing a strike base.

Another concern at the time that Robertson was about to depart for Nicaragua was the possibility that Guatemala, at least the ground training site, might be subject to an OAS inspection team; and in late November 1960 the prospects for an internal US training site for the Cuban Brigade was being investigated. Among the possible areas discussed were Fort Benning, Fort Bragg, the Belle-Chase Naval ammunition depot in Louisiana, Camp Johnson in Louisiana, and Camp Bullis in Texas. While the possibility of holding, and/or training of ground force troops within the continental United States was a subject for discussion, there appeared to be little question that the forward strike base would have to be outside of the continental United States; and Puerto Cabezas was consistently regarded as the most likely -- if not the only -- site for that strike base. 20/

Shortly prior to his departure for Nicaragua, Rip Robertson raised a series of pertinent questions which he hoped to have answered -- or at least discussed -- prior to his departure. Among the questions were several which clearly indicated Robertson's awareness of the political implications of the position

that he was assuming:

1. Am I cleared to speak frankly with local President and local Chief of Army as to US Government participation?

2. General but not specific operational concepts (example: we plan supplies and infiltrations until we can stir up something, and then we will support it with plenty of firepower).

3. Announcement of the number and type (resupply, bombing, strafing, etc.) air missions daily on the day it is to run?

4. When the local President asks for politics and identity of indigenous movement or movements we are supporting, do we tell him? (Where can I get a good briefing on this point?)

5. Have arrangements been made for reimbursement to local President abroad for expenditures he may assume for us? What do I tell him re this subject, at first meeting?* 21/

Also, as Robertson was about to depart, there

was considerable concern about the problem in Nicaragua

---

* Robertson also asked for guidance on the most pragmatic questions of contracting authority, cover, and base security -- particularly whether DPD would be subject to WH security practices even at the expense of air ops.

that was being raised with the Special Group, particularly the concerns of Assistant Secretary of State for American Republic Affairs, Thomas Mann. In an apparent response to a question raised by Mann, Chief, WH Division, sent a note to Mann on 1 December 1960, in which it was stated:

> As one of the actions to be taken in response to the Presidential and Special Group Meetings, we would proceed to survey, construct, and man a staging and refueling facility at Puerto Cabezas. This action is in accord with preliminary conversations with President Somoza. There would at no time be a substantial force at the installation, and no US personnel would be in the capital of the nation except one agency contract employee with long local experience, who would [   ] by dealing with the President on this operation.
>
> The initial survey team of 5-men would fly into Puerto Cabezas on or about 7 December. Subject to their findings it is expected that such minimum airstrip repairs and construction of temporary buildings would be completed by 15 January [1961]. 22/

The Agency presumption that it had been acting in response to the directive of the President and the wishes of the Special Group, apparently met with opposition from Mann; for in a handwritten note on a copy of the memorandum cited above, Dick Drain (Chief, WH/4/P&P) recorded:

Later that morning [2 December 1960], Devine called C/WH to say that Mann had referred the matter to [Livingston] Merchant and felt there had been no Special Group discussion or decision underlying the Nicaragua proposal. I called ADD/A who (after speaking w/C/WH) called Joe Scott to see where we stood. Scott said Merchant felt this was a matter for secretarial review. For this review, State would need more detail. Barnes undertook to provide same. Used [Thomas A.] Parrot to inform [Gordon] Gray and DOD and himself inform DCI. 23/*

In order to insure that the Special Group was properly notified, WH/4 prepared a memorandum on Nicaraguan aspects of the Cuban operation on 3 December 1960, and on 6 December 1960 another memorandum was prepared concerning several problems, among which was included that of the Nicaraguan strike base. These materials were forwarded for use at the Special Group meeting of 8 December 1960. 24/

Although formal sanction for his mission was still being debated, Robertson departed for Nicaragua

---

* Mr. Merchant was Under Secretary of State for Political Affairs, and Joseph W. Scott was his Special Assistant. Thomas A. Parrot served as Executive Secretary for the Special Group 5412, and Gordon Gray was President Eisenhower's National Security Adviser.

early in December, and [   ] was instructed that either he or the Ambassador should advise President Somoza about Robertson's role and arrange for an early meeting. 25/ On 8 December 1960, Robertson had his first meeting with President Luis Somoza and Noel Pallais Debayle, Somoza's cousin and contact man with JMATE. The purpose of this initial meeting was to establish his identity with Somoza and to arrange for the black flight for another survey team that was coming in to examine the Puerto Cabezas area. For all practical purposes, from this time forward until his departure in mid-February of 1961, the conduct of a major segment of US foreign policy was in the hands of a CIA contract employee -- the State representatives standing to one side as the Agency forged ahead with its anti-Castro program. 26/*

---

* Not only did the State representatives stand aside, but also [   ]. In his transmittal of Robertson's first reports, [   ] reported as follows:

> "CADICK [Robertson] is now operating completely outside of [   ]
> -- because [   ] wants to know nothing more than what is absolutely required that he know regarding these activities, he has given CADICK the essential cryptonyms, [   ]
>   (footnote continued on following page)

Prior to his first meeting with Somoza on
8 December 1960, Robertson did meet with Pallais on
7 December 1960, to make arrangements for the session
with Somoza. 28/. The delicate situation in which
Robertson found himself is quite evident from the
questions which were put to him by Pallais in his
initial meeting. The President's cousin pointed out
that Somoza would be pushing for a promise that "we
would back him, if and when he was caught in the act,"
and Robertson was faced with a similar question during
his session with Somoza. Rip straddled the line very
carefully and pointed out in all instances that he could
only express his own personal opinion and make quite
sure that the Nicaraguans understood that he had no
official verification that Somoza would be supported
in case of difficulties with other member states of

[President Luis Somoza],   [Gen-
eral Anastasio Somoza], and   [Noel
Pallais de Bayle], which he has memorized.
This has been done for his own and operational security. Hereafter   will receive CADICK's finished reports sealed
in an envelope." 27/

the OAS, the UN, or with Cuba. Robertson did play down the likelihood of serious military intervention by Cuba because of the strength of the Brigade's Air Force, once it moved into Nicaragua. 29/

The care with which Robertson was treading the line with Somoza is quite similar to the handling of the situation by Lou Napoli at the time of his visit to Nicaragua in mid-October of 1960. Napoli also avoided very carefully indicating that views that he expressed represented anything other than his own personal thoughts.*

---

* However, in a conversation with a member of WH Division on 9 August 1972, Napoli stated that he had assured the Somozas that the United States would not back out once the Cuban operation started and, further, that if Castro retaliated either militarily or in the UN/OAS, Somoza could expect full support from the US.

When the interviewer questioned Napoli about the authority that he had for making such statements, the response was that he had this from Headquarters. He further stated that he did not worry concerning the authority that Headquarters had. 30/

For whatever reason, Robertson's role in the negotiations with Somoza apparently left a bad after taste with Napoli, for in this same interview in 1972 he was quite pointed in noting that it was he, rather than Robertson who had played the principal role in negotiations with the head of the Nicaraguan state. 31/

(footnote continued on following page)

Robertson's on-going dialogue with Somoza continued through December, quite successfully from the standpoint of acceptance of Agency proposals for developing Puerto Cabezas. Robertson noted that aside from the political discussions which could not be escaped, every point raised by the engineering advance party was agreed to by Somoza. 32/

Even though the Agency's representative in Nicaragua was making good progress, the same apparently did not apply in Headquarters area. On 28 December 1960 the Chief of WH/4 was requesting action on the part of the A/DDP/A to get a formal policy decision. The question of the *quid pro quo's* requested by Somoza apparently had been put to Assistant Secretary Mann, and according to Chief, WH/4, Mann was

> rather cold on the subject, with the inevitable result that nothing had happened. I would appreciate, therefore, if you [C. Tracy Barnes, A/DDP/A] in your role as coordinator would take the matter up with Ambassador Willauer. We are now at the point that we must obligate funds and commence rehabilitation of JMTIDE if we are to meet the 15 February - 1 March deadline.

The record verifies that both Napoli and Robertson acted in a highly commendable manner during the touchy negotiations with the Central American dictator.

> Obviously, we cannot in good conscience
> expend government funds unless we have
> reasonable assurance that we can use the
> area. Given the absolute essentiality of
> JMTIDE to our operation, the need for
> early resolution is quite apparent. 33/

Despite the concern over the official policy for

Nicaragua, Headquarters apparently missed or ignored

one very important point made by Robertson in mid-

December 1960. It was a point which from project in-

ception until near the collapse of the Brigade was to

plague the JMARC operation. Robertson pointed out

that

> the real problem is that though all pre-
> liminary activities can be explained away
> by cover schemes devised thus far, we
> much face fact that once shooting starts,
> it is certain that JMTIDE will come to
> light for what it is. 34/

Had this comment been carefully considered at

this time, perhaps the whole question of plausible

deniability could have been laid out on the table or

laid to rest before it became a critical factor -- if

not *the* critical factor -- in modifying the operational

plan. While Robertson went about his business in

Nicaragua, there was an increasing flurry of activity

in the Headquarters area concerning the anti-Castro

movement; and the situation in Nicaragua was consistently introduced as a part of that on-going problem.

D. Qualms at High Levels

With reference to the use or non-use of the
Nicaraguan base -- a question which was still unanswered
at the turn of the year -- Tom Mann was looked on as
the villain in the piece by the Agency's representatives.
In preparing material for the DCI to use at a high
level meeting, Tracy Barnes indicated that Mann would
probably oppose the use of the Nicaraguan strike base.
Barnes argues that Mann would reason that since the
operation was essentially one backed by the United
States Government, the attempt to establish a covert
Agency operated base was improper. The United States
Government should openly admit its anti-Castro posture,
for continuation of the attempt to maintain covert
activities in Nicaragua and Guatemala would (in Mann's
thinking according to Barnes) jeopardize the already
somewhat shaky governments of Ydigoras and Somoza. 35/

In his memorandum noting Mann's position, Barnes
chose to ignore, or at least to pass over, the merits
of overt US intervention. Instead of looking at the

question in issue, he pointed out that the Agency's position was that unless bases in the US could be obtained, the only acceptable land mass from which we could fly the B-26's to strike Cuba was Puerto Cabezas. 36/

In preparing material for Barnes prior to a 5 January 1961 meeting of the Special Group, the Chief of WH/4, P&P, the hard-nosed, hard-talking Dick Drain noted an even more significant problem concerning the situation in Nicaragua. Drain pointed out that the Special Group in its meetings of 8 and 15 December had left a number of points hanging, including the authority to use the airstrip at Puerto Cabezas for spoiling raids and tactical air support, and in reference to those two meetings of the Special Group, Drain wrote:

> There was considerable discussion of the logistics timing involved in the development of the strip for strikes in the time framework of 15 Feb - 1 Mar. Even though the logistics factors alone would seem to make it necessary for the Group now to approve this facility for airstrikes, it was felt that the more basic question was the very approval of airstrikes. It was therefore agreed that this Special Group would be asked

to approve spoiling raids and tactical airstrikes from Puerto Cabezas beginning D-1. 37/*

Despite discussion of these issues, when Barnes prepared his background memorandum for the DCI to use at the 5 January meeting of the Special Group, the questions and problems which have just been mentioned were totally ignored! With reference to Puerto Cabezas, Barnes said that steps had been taken to prepare the strike base

> and we are planning to move to Puerto
> Cabezas substantial amounts of material
> [*sic*] starting around the 15th or 20th
> of January, including aviation ordnance,
> resupply ammo and weapons for ground
> forces, aviation gas, diesel fuel, and
> possibly some extra one-man packs,

although work on the base did not actually begin until late January or early February 1961. 38/**

------

* In view of what would subsequently become one of the most controversial issues concerning the whole Bay of Pigs operation -- the number and nature of the air-strikes -- it is interesting to note the reference at this early date to D-1 air activity.

** On 11 Jan 61 according to one source, a Headquarters team arrived at JMTIDE to arrange for and supervise the construction; and Rip Robertson was notified to report to Headquarters on 27 January 1961 "for participation JMCLEAR planning for JMTIDE construction." 39/ The Chief, WH/4, PM, Col. Jack Hawkins also noted on 4 January 1961 that "necessary construction and repairs at this base are now scheduled to commence." 40/

Completely ignoring the issue of authorization for use
of Puerto Cabezas or the question of permission for
airstrikes which had previously been brought to his
attention, Barnes chose to focus on the economics and
the potential loss of US inventories which might be
moved into Puerto Cabezas and lost -- that is, appropriated by Somoza -- if the decision should be made
either to move the training activity to United States
bases and/or to back off from the use of the Nicaraguan
air base. What motivated Barnes to suggest this approach
is unknown; and in view of the real problems requiring
decisions it was a unbelievable performance.

Even as the Agency was seeking policy guidance
with respect to utilization of Puerto Cabezas, Robertson alerted Headquarters that the Nicaraguan situation
would soon be complicated by requests from the Government of Nicaragua for a $(US) 2 million loan to rebuild
motor and railroads which had recently been flooded --
a request which the Nicaraguan Ambassador Oscar Sevilla-
Sacasa would present to the Department of State. In
addition, a Development Loan fund of $(US) 8 million
was also pending. 41/ When General Anastasio Somoza --

President Somoza's brother -- came to the United States
to attend the Kennedy inauguration, he also met with
Allen Dulles to discuss the problem of JMTIDE and of
continued US support for Nicaragua. At the same time,
the General also pressed the DCI for assistance in
obtaining the loans that were just mentioned. The
DCI however pointed Somoza toward the Department of
State, suggesting that Assistant Secretary Thomas Mann
was the logical contact for discussing loans. 42/

The question of the *quid-pro-quo* of loans for
Nicaragua in return for the utilization of Puerto
Cabezas continued through February, with the Chief
WH/4 and the Chief, WH Division both playing active
roles in attempting to get a commitment from State
for the $2 million loan -- and State support for the
$8 million World Bank loan. 43/ On the last day of
February 1961, a proposal from Chief, Western Hemisphere
Division to the DCI suggesting that the DDP, the DDCI,
or the DCI "press the Department of State for favorable
action in Nicaragua's two pending loans" was signed
and approved at least through the DDP level. Whether
the DCI actually approved this recommendation is a

moot point and one which was not clarified even subsequent to the close out of the JMATE operation. 44/

At the same time that he was suggesting that pressure be put on the Department of State to assist Nicaragua in obtaining the loans, Chief, WHD also was recommending that Ambassador Whelan be designated to discuss Project JMATE with President Somoza. Col. King, in speaking of Whelan remarked as follows:

> His relationship with President Somoza makes him an ideal representative to convey assurances that the project will be implemented, will continue until Castro's defeat, and be conducted with US awareness of Nicaragua's contribution and with support for her position should the operation produce pressures on her in the UN, the OAS, or otherwise. Should it not be possible to extend such assurances during Ambassador Whelan's availability, then such assurances should be extended by a representative of the US government as soon as possible thereafter. 45/*

E. Back to Robertson -- Activist with Foresight

While negotiations over the formalities of the use of Puerto Cabezas, dragged on at Headquarters,

---

* To the author's knowledge, the suggestion for a commitment to support the project "until Castro's defeat" was never officially made to either President Somoza or President Ydigoras nor to the anti-Castro Cuban political or military leaders.

Robertson, on the scene in Nicaragua, made solid progress in establishing a base at JMTIDE. Between 3 and
17 January 1961, for example, he reported on three
meetings with General Anastasio Somoza; and in the
course of these, made arrangements for the movement
of guards into the TIDE area in anticipation of the
arrival of the first supply ship toward the end of
January 1961. He also worked out arrangements for
housing and paying the *guardia nacional* contingent
which would be responsible for base security; and he
set up the bookkeeping for the expenditures for the
guardia. Although he gave no specifics, Robertson
indicated that he had set up a system for alerting
JMTIDE when "doubtful persons or newspapermen board
the local airlines," and apparently this system was
considerably more successful than the program established for the JMADD and JMTRAV activities. 46/*

With reference to the security problem, Robertson
reported that the arrival of the team reponsible for

---

* In this context Rip did note that he was being
"pestered" by Cora Waterhouse, a newspaper woman
from the United States who was trying to find out
what was going on.

supervising the re-creation of Puerto Cabezas tipped the local Americans off as to who was behind the activity at the airfield. Rip was particularly high in his praise of the Agency engineer who both reduced the time for getting the operation in order and also had saved money in the process. In reporting on his activities through mid-January Robertson made one complaint which he voiced as follows:

> In the future, I would suggest that the size of such groups be cut to a minimum. There is something uncommon about a group of four men, of whom only one is occupied (to the eyes of observers) and only one of which knows the business for which they are there. In reality, one engineer would accomplish all that is being done at TIDE with the exception of course, of commo. 47/

In terms of security at JMTIDE, Robertson also had some other problems which he seemed to have handled very well, especially considering that they concerned US military representatives in Nicaragua. The Chief of the US Military Assistance Group to Guatemala, in the course of an inspection of National Guard facilities, had come into the TIDE area; and upon his return to Managua had prepared a report on the activities and installation. The US Ambassador requested that this

report not be forwarded to Washington, but as a result
of the trip, the Military Attache and the Air Attache
in Managua got the hots to trot down to TIDE. Ambassador Whelan, however, backed Robertson's request
that such trips be denied; but fearing that the Ambassador would be unable to contain future requests from
the Department of Defense representatives, Robertson
asked Headquarters for assistance. On 1 February 1961,
a cable went to Robertson from Headquarters stating
"Headquarters has arranged with Pentagon superiors
Mil Attache and MAAG Chief to send them today orders
neither visit nor report on JMTIDE". 48/*

Rip Robertson performed yeoman service in his
stint in Nicaragua in the early months of 1961. In

---

* An additional problem with a US military contingent
apparently was headed off when the Agency requested
the Pentagon to scrub the planned visit of an Army Map
Service NIS (National Intelligence Survey) group to
TIDE. 49/ Toward mid-June 1961 the arrangements which
the Agency had made through the Subsidiary Division,
Joint Staff and Assistant Chief of Staff, Intelligence,
US Army still held. At that time (12 June 1961), however, the Agency did authorize access to JMTIDE to US
military personnel who were involved in decisions concerning disposal of the materiel still stockpiled at
Puerto Cabezas. 49a/

addition to what has already been noted, his relationships with the Somozas -- President and General --
were carried on in a direct and friendly manner. If
the situation demanded, there was no hesitation on
Robertson's part to make a direct approach to President Somoza. Based on reports of these meetings, it
is clear that Robertson was regarded as the de-facto
representative re US foreign policy in Nicaragua.
Robertson reported, however, that he always emphasized
to the Nicaraguan leaders that his opinions were not
necessarily those of the USG. By the same token,
Robertson made clear that he would forward Somoza's
views to the proper authorities in the US Government.
Even though the United States had an Ambassador in
Nicaragua who was quite friendly with Somoza, Robertson's knowledgeability about the Agency's anti-Castro
operations really made him the key figure in the on-
going relationships between Nicaragua and the United
States.

With his detailed knowledge of the operational
plans for Puerto Cabezas, Robertson was in a much
better position to understand and appreciate Somoza's

desire for a more formal commitment for the United

States than he had received by mid-February of 1961.

In a lengthy exit session with Robertson at the time

of his departure (14 February 1961), the Nicaraguan

President emphasized how difficult it would be for

him to survive his pro-Castro opponents once Robertson

and Ambassador Whelan -- who was being replaced --

had both departed the country, unless the United States

provided him with some greater guarantees of support

for his assistance in the USG's anti-Castro activities.

As Somoza put it to Robertson, "I need to meet a man

who can say he just left Mr. Kennedy, and Mr. Kennedy

sends assurances that we are all in this together." 50/*

   When Robertson departed Nicaragua for Headquarters

on 14 February 1961, he received high marks from all

sources. [   ] cabled back as follows:

----

* Robertson noted that Somoza in response to a question concerning whether Mr. Dulles was of sufficient
stature to give the proper assurances responded "that
certainly Mr. Dulles was of stature enough to be able
to assure him, but as he (Somoza) had pointed out to
his brother, General A. Somoza, Mr. Dulles had talked
'only in generalities' to the General, and had avoided
the main issue." This was with reference to the
General's visit to the US at the time of the Kennedy
inaugural. 51/

desires commend Robertson for
excellent presentation and accomplishment
mission. Robertson's detached objective
approach, vis-a-vis Somoza. Ambassador and
underlined positive results. 52/*

F. Who Would Do What for Whom?

Robertson's suggestions for discussions were
taken to heart in Nicaragua and in Washington. Almost
immediately upon his departure, a series of cables
indicate that meetings were held between the President
of Nicaragua and Ambassador Whelan and, in Washington,
between Lou Napoli and Ambassador Sevilla-Sacasa. A
principal subject of the conversation was the status
of Nicaragua's pending loan applications to the USG
and the DLF. In neither Managua nor Washington did
Nicaragua get any commitment that the loans were going

---

* It should not be inferred from the foregoing that
all of Robertson's activities were devoted to hand-
holding with the Somozas. He got down to the very
nitty-gritty things directly related to the planned
operation against Fidel Castro, concerning himself
with such matters as port security, planning for
fueling and watering the vessels which would be used
to transport the Brigade to Cuba, and, probably, to
negotiating an agreement with Nicaragua to dispose of
the Brigade dead resulting from the invasion. One
knowledgeable source recalled that an arrangement was
made whereby the bodies would be transported to Nicaragua by boat or air, and that Somoza had offered to
give them a hero's burial. 53/

to be approved or authorized; but it was quite clear
that the Agency wished to defer to State on the matter
of the formal loan applications and to put the political
burden on the Department's back. 54/ At the same time
that the Agency was holding Somoza's hand, Headquarters
was being extremely concerned that none of our assurances
to Nicaragua got put into writing. 55/

On a very local level, Somoza pointed out to
Ambassador Whelan that because the government of Nicaragua had diverted funds which had been appropriated
by the Nicaraguan Congress to keep the railroad and road
systems operating in order to support TIDE activities,
he was going to be in a very embarrassing position
should TIDE collapse, and should the US fail to provide
the $(US)2 million loan. 56/ In Washington, Ambassador
Sevilla-Sacasa pressed Napoli for assistance in getting
high level assurance that Nicaragua would not suffer
in either the UN or OAS because of her anti-Castro
position. Sevilla-Sacasa suggested that Berle, Rusk,
or President Kennedy would be a suitable US spokesman
to indicate that Nicaragua's position would be supported
should any international or regional sanctions be

threatened for assistance given the Brigade by Nicaragua should the invasion of Cuba take place. 57/

As the date for the invasion approached -- and with the approval of Jake Esterline and C. Tracy Barnes -- Lou Napoli was reassigned (27 March 1961) to Managua on TDY to maintain personal contact with both President and General Somoza on the upcoming operation insofar as it might affect the Nicaraguan government; and like his predecessor, Rip Robertson, Napoli was to confine his activities to Managua and avoid JMTIDE. Napoli expected to do a certain amount of hand-holding on the matter of the loans and make reassuring noises without any firm commitments; and, similarly, he hoped to be able to assure the Nicaraguan government that it would receive support from the US should their Latin American neighbors take umbrage at Somoza's anti-Castro posture. Probably the most significant duty he was to undertake upon his return to Nicaragua was to brief Somoza on the upcoming military operation without, of course, revealing the strike date -- in fact, the instruction indicated that Napoli himself would not know the exact date. 58/

Among the points outlined in his scenario for the military briefing of Somoza, the following items are worth mention in view of the situation as it actually evolved. With reference to the Cuban Brigade members, it was to be emphasized that once they were on the ships they would never return to Nicaragua. With reference to the air strikes, the scenario stated:

> Air strikes will begin once landings [are] made and will continue until Castro knocked out. Fifteen B-26's will be used. Somoza need not worry about Cuban Air Force following the B-26's, as the mission of those planes in [sic] the total destruction of the Cuban Air Force. The success of the operation hinges largely on the continued uninterrupted use of TIDE for strategic and logistical support for rebels. Once we start, we must go until Castro falls. 59/

Despite the fact that Lou Napoli talked rather glibly about promises and assurances that should be given to Somoza, Jack Hawkins, Chief, WH/4/PM, in testifying to the Taylor Committee made the point that neither the Agency nor the USG ever gave Somoza a high level promise of support as a condition for use of Puerto Cabezas. In fact, Hawkins emphasized that up until the last moment, the use of this base might have been denied at the whim of Somoza. 60/

The situation was complicated by the fact that Washington was sitting on its hands waiting for a policy decision to implement the operational phase of JMTIDE; and this was further complicated by the question of the utilization of US military personnel at the Nicaragua base. As pointed out in the discussion of the Agency's relationships with the Government of Guatemala,* Jake Esterline had been forced to negotiate an agreement which, in effect, was a Status of Forces Agreement with the Government of Guatemala before permission was granted for the use of US Army Special Forces personnel at the ground training base, JMTRAV. When it was time to consider the initiation of operations at Puerto Cabezas, the question of utilization of US personnel in a foreign area again came up.

In early March 1961, a memorandum to the DDP from the Assistant Director for Operations, Office of Special Operations, Department of Defense, stated in part:

> The services and the Joint Staff have all reaffirmed that the Department of Defense policy established for Guatemala must apply to Nicaragua in the same manner. This subject has been discussed with the

---

* See Part I of this volume, pp. 57 ff.

Deputy Secretary of Defense by Brigadier
General Lansdale with a proposal that it
be raised at the next Group meeting. 61/

The end result was that neither Army Special Forces
nor USAF assignees were officially permitted to move
from Guatemalan bases to TIDE. The number of USAF
ground crew personnel who were at TIDE "unofficially"
cannot be determined.

G. Down to the Wire with Somoza

Whether or not, adequate formal assurance of support in the OAS or UN was actually reached between
President Somoza and high level officials of the United
States Government is uncertain -- what is certain, however, is that Somoza gave his full cooperation to the
Agency effort to mount the operation out of Puerto
Cabezas. As of 10 April, in a meeting with the Agency
representative, it was made clear that the Somozas
were going to do everything in their power to insure
the security of the operation. Measures to be taken
included the monitoring and censorship of radio, outgoing cables, international telephones, television,
and the press, and control of the airlines -- on 15 April
1961, for example, commercial air traffic to Puerto

Cabezas and all other air traffic, except for Agency operated aircraft, would be completely prohibited. 62/

Somoza also was going to go so far as to make an announcement on 15 April that the activity which certainly would be known to be taking place at Puerto Cabezas was in response to the threat of possible incursions from Costa Rica and the need to have the Nicaraguan military forces in a state of readiness. 63/ At the same time that this cover story was being discussed with the representatives of the Nicaraguan Government, General Somoza was visiting TIDE and spoke with Colonels Hawkins and Gaines who were in Puerto Cabezas to give the final briefings prior to the beginning of operations; and Somoza raised the question of possible attacks by Castro's Air Force should any of his planes get off the ground. The Agency's representatives regarded this as a legitimate concern; and even though convinced that Castro's FAR (Fuerza Aerea Revolucionario) would be destroyed on the ground, they asked Headquarters to approach the US Navy about establishing a radar picket operation off the Nicaraguan coast to relay warnings of incoming Castro aircraft.

The picket would not only assuage Somoza's fears, but would be insurance against any unorthodox surprise attack on TIDE.* The emergency cable from TIDE to Headquarters recommended that the radar picket be established by 0800 local time 15 April 1961, or as soon as possible thereafter; and it also suggested that instructions be provided for communications to link the Navy picket with both TIDE and Managua. 64/

One of the few points of contention between the Agency representatives and the highest officials of the Nicaraguan government occurred at the time that the operation was being mounted at Puerto Cabezas. One of the Garcia Lines ships -- the *Lake Charles* which was to be one of the backup ships of the invasion fleet -- arrived in Puerto Cabezas where 10 of her Cuban crew members were detained as potential pro-Castro security risks. These crew members were re-moved from the *Lake Charles* and turned over to Captain

_____

* The idea suggested by General Somoza -- that bombs might be rolled out the doors of Cubana airlines C-47's or other transport aircraft -- undoubtedly struck a familiar note with the air ops people at TIDE. After all, they had tried to develop a make-shift napalm bomb to be rolled out -- or dropped out on a pallet -- of a C-46 or C-54. (See Volume I, Air Operations.)

Quintana, the commander of the Nicaraguan Gardia
Nacional unit which was the security force for TIDE;
and then they were confined to some of the nearby
military barracks. 65/ As early as January 1961,
General Somoza had told Robertson that Nicaragua would
provide detention facilities for any of the Cubans who
proved to be "reluctant warriors" when it was time to
embark for the invasion. 65a/ This action, however,
apparently did not fit the case or else it had not
been cleared properly with General Somoza for a cable
from TIDE to Headquarters reported that General Somoza
had visited TIDE on 13 April and "in strong terms ordered
removal from JMTIDE immediately 14 detainees currently
in custody Capt. Quintana." 66/*

The order for the immediate removal of the Cubans
who were being held under guard of the Nicaraguan

---

* The only explanation for the discrepancy in the number of detainees is that there were additional Cubans
who had been pulled out of the Brigade units when they
were being embarked at Puerto Cabezas. The figure of
10 from the *Lake Charles* comes from a Havana news release attributed to one of the detainees. 66a/ As of
25 April 1961, the crewmen were still in custody, and
Headquarters instructed TIDE to release them ASAP to
the Captain of either the *Lake Charles* or the *Atlantico*. 66b/

troops was apparently rescinded, for on 22 April a cable from Managua to Washington indicated that President Somoza had approved delaying the removal of the Cubans until 24 April. Somoza himself was characterized as continuing to be quite cooperative with the Agency representatives but fearful that with the reopening to commercial air traffic of Puerto Cabezas that the detainees in TIDE would be discovered and consequently his cover story for TIDE activities would be exposed. 67/ In any event, the Cubans who were being held prisoner were returned to the United States aboard the *Atlantico* which, upon the collapse of the invasion, had returned to Puerto Cabezas and thence to the US via Key West, Norfolk, and Baltimore. From the last port, the prisoners were then sent to Washington, and from Washington on down to Miami and thence to Cuba. 68/*

---

* The Agency's relations with Nicaragua also became somewhat strained because Miro Cardona was never brought to Nicaragua to meet with President Somoza, despite the fact that this had been requested by Somoza on several occasions. Why Headquarters was so reluctant to approve such a meeting is, in hindsight, difficult to understand. Just prior to moving the operation from Guatemala to Nicaragua, Miro Cardona was completing a tour of the TRAV/MADD installations. Why he could not have been taken on to the JMTIDE area at that time is not made clear in either the cable traffic or other data that are available. 69/

As an appropriate final note to indicate the dominant role of the Agency in determining US foreign policy vis-a-vis Nicaragua, a cable of 15 April 1961 from Managua to Headquarters reads as follows:

> Napoli requests know, if Ambassador Brown, who ETA Managua 16 April, briefed on JMATE/JMTIDE. If not, does Headquarters authorize briefing if Ambassador so requests. 70/.

This was a strange question to have to be asked of Washington at this particular time. Even stranger, perhaps, is the fact that the Department of State was scheduling a new Ambassador to arrive at the time that the planned attack on Cuba -- out of the country to which he was being assigned -- was about to kick off. Whether this was an indication of relative indifference on the part of the Department or a sign of supreme confidence in the ability of its personnel to cope is left to the reader's judgment.

H. Postscript on Nicaragua

Two interesting postscripts to the story of the Agency's involvement in Nicaraguan foreign policy concern the period following the collapse of the invasion. In May 1961, Lou Napoli was informed by former Ambassador

Whelan that Somoza, through Ambassador Sevilla-Sacasa, expressed the opinion that Napoli had not kept him properly informed regarding the military activities at the time of the invasion. In the memorandum of his conversation with Whelan, Napoli pointed out that this undoubtedly was true because he, himself, had not been informed immediately of the developing military situation; and, in fact, it was through Captain Quintana of the Nicaraguan Guardia Nacional at TIDE that he first learned that the beach at Playa Girón was being abandoned.

Moreover, Napoli pointed out that the Agency had violated its own commitment to Somoza that none of the Brigade wounded would be brought back into the TIDE area -- a commitment that Napoli had made to President Somoza after receiving prior Headquarters guidance. Further, the Agency failed to meet the date that it had agreed to for removing those wounded. In addition some of the vessels returning to TIDE from Cuba had wounded aboard, but through Napoli's efforts, apparently, they were not off-loaded. Somoza apparently bore no ill will toward Napoli, for upon the latter's departure, the President told him that he looked forward to his return. Napoli, in the hope of maintaining the close and supportive relationship with the Nicaraguan President, expressed the desire to be able -- in the future -- to pass on full and complete details of planned activities that might relate to Nicaragua. 71/

The other postscript concerns the apparent reluctance of newly appointed Ambassador Brown to step on the Agency's toes. In June 1961, the Agency had apparently evolved a plan for using some of the Cuban pilots who had been trained during Project JMATE as instructors for the Nicaraguan Air Force. Ambassador Brown in objecting to this, requested that the following message be sent CIA:

> Now that Cuban invasion is over and we are closing out the NIC operation, it seems to me that we should not open up the possibility of raising future problems or bad local press by bringing back Cuban exiles as instructors. It seems we could avoid all chance of adverse local reaction by the use of already existing mechanisms such as Col. Hardee and his unit which capable of doing good job. I would not like to hamper progress of negotiations, but I would like to express the opinion, based on my present knowledge of the situation, that I would prefer no Cubans be used as instructors. 72/

The rather cautious wording of the cable which the Ambassador asked to be sent to the Agency indicates that he apparently was aware that the Agency more than his own Department was conducting the close out of activities vis-a-vis the Nicaraguan government, particularly the question of what materiel would be turned over to the Somozas.

Part III

Conclusions

In the instances of both Guatemala and Nicaragua from the Spring of 1960 until the Spring of 1961, it has been shown that Agency personnel involved in Project JMATE were the principal figures in the on-going relations between those countries and the US Government. In the instance of Guatemala, the US Ambassador for all practical purposes became "inoperative"; and in Nicaragua the opposite condition prevailed -- anything that the Agency suggested received ambassadorial blessing. Neither extreme was desirable; and in both instances what the Chief Executive of each country most wished to avoid -- that it become known that his country provide a base for the anti-Castro Cubans -- became unavoidable.

That the relationship between each nation and the US could be "plausibly denied" when the concept of the anti-Castro plan shifted from guerrilla type operations to invasion was a snare and delusion. That the White House and the Department of State were prayerful that the USG would not be criticized by the UN or the OAS

as a partner in crime was similarly wishful. The one
voice of reason in Washington was that of Thomas Mann,
Assistant Secretary of State for Latin American Affairs;
and it was Mann who from the fall of 1960 until he was
replaced in 1961 railed against the failure of the US
to abandon plausible deniability and openly support an
anti-Castro program with use of arms. Unfortunately
Mann won no converts. In the end, he, too, played
the game.

The question that will always remain unanswered
is whether the whole shooting match at the BOP might
have been cancelled if the Department of State representatives in either Guatemala or Nicaragua had been
better qualified and had been given better guidance
from Washington about the fact that there could not
be degrees of plausible deniability -- either the
operation was deniable or it was not. If it was not
-- and it obviously was not -- an alert and forceful
Ambassador might have precipitated a decision either
to stand down the operation or to openly support the
Brigade.

Source References*

Part I

Guatemala

1. Cox, Alfred T., *Paramilitary Ground Activities at the Staff Level, 15 September 1955 - 31 December 1961.* [   ] Mar 70. Vol. I, pp. 81-85.

2. Memo for DCI from J. C. King, 29 Feb 60, sub: What We Are Doing in Cuba.

3. Revision of General Covert Action Plan for Cuba by C. Tracy Barnes, 14 Mar 60.

3a. Schlesinger, Arthur M., Jr., *A Thousand Days* (Boston: Houghton Mifflin, 1965), p. 228. U.**

4. Cable for Director from Guatemala, 31 May 60, GUAT 811 (IN 45788).

   Memo for Record from Jacob D. Esterline, 20 Jun 60, sub: Negotiations with President Miguel Ydigoras Fuentes re Use of Guatemalan Terrain for JMARC Operations.

4a. State: Incoming Telegram to Sec State from Guatemala City, 18 May 60, Control No. 13560.

5. MR from Jacob D. Esterline, 8 Jun 60, sub: Meeting with Roberto Alejos, Personal Representative of President Ydigoras Fuentes of Guatemala.

---

* Unless otherwise specified all sources are classified SECRET. A copy of, or a note on, each of the references cited herein is filed in the CIA History Staff under HS/HC 2632 "Source References, BOP History."

** All subsequent references to commercial publications (books, magazines, and newspapers) are UNCLASSIFIED.

6. Cable ETAT Roberto Alejos, Embaguate Washington,
    D. C. 526, RCI YW190 WN/GU234 Guatemala via
    Tropical 54 GUATGOVT 7[60]1834. U.

7. Cable for Director from MASH, 15 Jun 60, MASH 0063
    (IN 11927).

    MR from Casimiro Barquin, 22 Jun 60, sub: Trip
    Report -- Miami to Guatemala City and Return.

8. Same as Source 7.

9. Same as Source 7.

10. Cables to Director from Guatemala, 6 Jul 60,
    GUAT 891 (IN 20434) and 21 Jun 60, GUAT 855
    (IN 14802).

11. Not used.

12. Not used.

13. Cables to Director: from TRAV 12 Jul 60, TRAV 003
    (IN 23432); from Guatemala 23 Jul 60, GUAT 944
    (IN 28495) and 30 Jul 60, GUAT 965 (IN 31262).

14. Office of Logistics, Engineering Staff, RECD,
    Agency Engineering Activity, 1947-66, DDS/HS OL-11,
    Vol. I, 63-67; Vol. II, 132-193, Feb 72.

15. *Ibid.*, Vol. I, pp. 55.

16. Cables: To Guatemala from Director, 5 Aug 60,
    DIR 44035 (OUT 55613); tò Director from JMTRAV,
    7 Aug 60, TRAV 009 (IN 34609); to Director from
    Guatemala, 27 Aug 60, GUAT 124 (IN 44288).

17. Daily Progress Reports -- Support, 5 Aug 60.
    Job 63-42, Folder 7.

18. Cable to Director from Guatemala, 8 Sep 60, GUAT
    192 (IN 49342).

18a. Daily Log -- PM Section, 8 Dec 60 (Daily Progress
Reports -- PM, Jun 60 - Mar 61).

19. Cables: To Director from TRAV, 5 Dec 60, TRAV
0171 (IN 12064); to JMTRAV from Director, 8 Dec 60,
DIR 15481 (OUT 50885); to Bell from Guatemala,
7 Jan 61, GUAT 789 (IN 1124).

20. Cable to Director from Guatemala, 6 Oct 60, GUAT
362 (IN 23228).

21. Cables: To Director from Guatemala, 7 Sep 60,
GUAT 190 (IN 49039); to Guatemala from Director,
9 Sep 60, DIR 49902 (OUT 68098); to Guatemala
from Director, 16 Sep 60, DIR 00989 (OUT 70502).

22. Cables: To Director from Guatemala, 13 Sep 60,
GUAT 232 (IN 11587); to Director from CINCLANFLT,
20 Sep 60, CITE 038 (IN 15111); to Director from
Guatemala, 20 Oct 60, GUAT 414 (IN 30311).

23. Cables: To Director from Guatemala, 8 Sep 60,
GUAT 192 (IN 49342); to Guatemala from Director,
9 Sep 60, DIR 49839 (OUT 68022).

Daily Progress Reports -- Support, 19 Sep 60.
Job 63-42, Folder 7.

24. Cable to Director from Guatemala, 11 Sep 60,
GUAT 231 (IN 11074).

25. *Ibid.*, 6 Oct 60, GUAT 360 (IN 23292).

25a. Russo`, Andrew J., *Air Support of Cuban Operations
1960-62*, pp. 58-62. (Draft MSS. HS/CSG 2627).

26. MR from Joseph F. Langan, 23 Sep 60, sub: JMADD
Security Incident.

26a. Job 64-739, Box 1. File: [   ] - PM.

27. Cable to Director from JMADD, 10 Sep 60, MADD 0026
(IN 10581).

28. Cables to Director from MADD: 8 Oct 60, MADD 0205
    (IN 24370); 9 Oct 60, MADD 0212 (IN 24738);
    11 Oct 60, MADD 0214 (IN 25364); 13 Oct 60,
    MADD 0237 (IN 26794).

29. Memo for Chief, WH Division from J. D. Esterline,
    21 Oct 60, sub: Authority to Obligate $150,000
    for JMARC PM Activities -- JMADD Land Compensation.

30. Cable to Director from Guatemala, 4 Nov 60,
    GUAT 463 (IN 37955).

31. *Ibid.*, 25 Nov 60, GUAT 599 (IN 47673).

    Cable to Guatemala from Director, 26 Nov 60,
    DIR 13543 (OUT 96600).

32. Cables to Bell from Guatemala: 13 Apr 61, GUAT
    1254 (IN 3135); 31 Apr 61, GUAT 1255 (IN 3137).

    Cable to Guatemala from Bell, 17 Apr 61, BELL
    4642 (OUT 6803).

33. Dispatches to Chief, WHD from ▢ Guatemala City:
    9 Aug 60, sub: JMARC: Use of Alias by Guatemalan
    Contact; 3 Feb 61, sub: Engagement of ▢
    as Independent Contractor.

34. Dispatch to Chief, WHD from ▢ Guatemala, 9 Aug 60,
    sub: Justification for Use of Guatemalan Engineer
    at JMTRAV.

    Cables: To Guatemala from Bell: 14 Jan 61, BELL
    0530 (OUT 6579); to Bell from Guatemala, 7 Apr 61,
    GUAT 1226 (IN 2140); to Bell from Guatemala,
    12 Apr 61, GUAT 1243 (IN 2922).

35. Memo for DCI from J. C. King, 21 Oct 60, sub:
    Observations on Briefing of Assistant Secretary
    of State Thomas Mann re JMARC/Guatemala Operations
    on 20 Oct 60.

36. Oral History Interview: Jacob D. Esterline by
    Jack B. Pfeiffer, 10-11 Nov 75, Tape 4, p. 51. U.*

---

* This and all other Oral History Interviews, all con-
versations, and all correspondence conducted by Jack B.
Pfeiffer are UNCLASSIFIED.

37. Cables to Director from Guatemala; 22 Jul 60,
    GUAT 938 (IN 28195) and 24 Jul 60, GUAT 943
    (IN 28530).

    State: Incoming Telegrams to Sec State from
    Guatemala City: 19 Jul 60, Control No. 13308;
    20 Jun 60, No. 37. C.

37a. Dispatch from Chief, WHD, 3 Oct 60, sub: JMARC/
    Administrative/Instructions for Bernard M. Parks.
    [?]-301.

38. Cables: To Guatemala from Director, 8 Nov 60,
    DIR 10654 (OUT 90384); to Director from Guatemala,
    12 Oct 60, GUAT 389 (IN 25980); to Director from
    MADD, 31 Oct 60, MADD 0434 (IN 35850); to Director
    from MADD, 1 Nov 60, MADD 0444 (IN 35917); to
    Director from Guatemala, 1 Nov 60, GUAT 445 (IN
    35899); to JMADD/JMTRAV from Director, 15 Oct 60,
    DIR 06269 (OUT 81460).

39. Cable to Director from MADD, 13 Nov 60, MADD 0539
    (IN 41791).

39a. State: Incoming Telegram to Sec State from Guate-
    mala City, 13 Nov 60, No. 222. U.

39b. Memo for Chief, WH from Richard Helms, 18 Nov 60,
    sub: US Naval Patrol in the Caribbean.

39c. Oral History Interview: Billy B. Campbell by
    Jack B. Pfeiffer, 15 Jun 76, Tape 1A, p. 10.

39d. Discussion between Sidney Stembridge and Jack B.
    Pfeiffer, 12 May 76 and telecon 17 May 76, sub:
    Alejos Violation of Commo Area JMADD, 13 Nov 60.

40. Cable to Director from Guatemala, 14 Nov 60, GUAT
    522 (IN 41922).

41. Oral History Interview: Richard M. Bissell by
    Jack B. Pfeiffer, 17 Oct 75, Tape 2, p. 25.

42. Cable to Director from Guatemala, 14 Nov 60, GUAT 526 (IN 42903).

43. Cable to Director from Guatemala, 17 Nov 60, GUAT 567 (IN 44141).

44. Letter from C. W. Seigrist to Jack B. Pfeiffer, 20 May 76. U.

45. Cable to Director from Guatemala, 14 Nov 60, GUAT 526 (IN 42903).

State: Incoming Telegram to Sec State from Guatemala City, 14 Nov 60, No. 226. U.

[T. A. Parrott], Special Group Meetings – Cuba, 16 Nov 60.

45a. Taylor Committee Report: MR's of PM Study Group Meetings, 7th Mtg, 1 May 61, p. 3.

MR from Casimiro Barquin, 14 Nov 60, sub: Support of JMADD, JMTRAV, and Other Elements in Guatemala. (JMC-0131).

46. Letter from Seigrist to Pfeiffer, *op. cit.*

47. Esterline-Pfeiffer OH Int., *op. cit.*, Tape 1, p. 20.

48. *Ibid.*, p. 18.

49. Cables to Guatemala from Director: 14 Nov 60, DIR 11290 (OUT 91822) and 14 Nov 60, DIR 11299 (OUT 91846).

50. Cable to Guatemala from Director, 14 Nov 60, DIR 11299 (OUT 91846).

50a. MR from Casimiro Barquin, 14 Nov 60 (JMC-0131), *op. cit.*

50b. MR from John F. Mallard, 14 Nov 60, sub: Conference with Department of Defense Representatives.

50c. Memo for Asst. to the Sec Def, OSO from Jacob
D. Esterline, 16 Nov 60, sub: Emergency Evacuation Assistance.

MR from Richard D. Drain, 21 Nov 60, sub: JMARC
Meeting with DDP.

51. *Ibid.*, DIR 11304 (OUT 91871).

52. Cables: To Director from Guatemala, 14 Nov 60,
GUAT 526 (IN 42093); to Guatemala-JMTRAV-JMADD
from Director, 14 Nov 60, DIR 11319 (OUT 91906). .

State, Incoming Telegram to Sec State from Guate-
mama City, 25 Nov 60, No. 262. TS.

53. Cable to Guatemala from Director, 14 Nov 60,
DIR 11343 (OUT 91978). TS.

53a. *Ibid.*

54. Cable to LA Stations from Director, 14 Nov 60,
DIR 11416 (OUT 92077).

55. Cables to Director from Guatemala: 25 Nov 60,
GUAT 602 (IN 47786); 29 Nov 60, GUAT 611 (IN
48900); 15 Dec 60, GUAT 709 (IN 17807).

56. State, Incoming Telegrams to Sec State from
Guatemala City: 31 May 60, Control No. 22443,
OUO; 14 Oct 60, No. 174, C; 17 Nov 60, No. 240.
C.

MR from John F. Mallard, 21 Nov 60, sub: Meeting
of SWGC. Job 63-42, Folder 1.

57. Cable to Guatemala from Director, 21 Nov 60,
DIR 12667 (OUT 94811).

58. Cable to Director from Guatemala, 22 Nov 60,
GUAT 583 (IN 46366).

59. Cable to Guatemala, JMASH, Havana et al, from
Director, 30 Nov 60, DIR 14227 (OUT 98163).

60. Cable to Director from JMTRAV, 9 Dec 60, TRAV 0182 (IN 14725).

61. Cable to Director from Guatemala, 10 Dec 60, GUAT 678 (IN 15261).

61a. Campbell-Pfeiffer OH Int., *op. cit.*, Tape 1A, pp. 7-8.

62. Cox, *Paramilitary Ground Activities, op. cit.*, Vol. II, pp. 388-391.

63. [ ] [ ] , Feb 69, pp. 29-31.

64. Memo for Chief, WH/4 from Col. J. Hawkins, 19 Oct 60, sub: Employment of Army Special Forces Training Cadres at TRAV.

    Memo for DDP from J. C. King, 28 Oct 60, sub: Employment of U.S. Army Special Forces for Training PM Cadres. (DD/P 0-5722).

    Memo for Chief, WH/4 from Richard M. Bissell, Jr., 7 Nov 60, sub: Employment of US Army Special Forces for Training PM Cadres. (DD/P 0-5861).

    Memo for MMPD from J. C. King, 16 Nov 60, sub: Requirement for US Army Special Forces Personnel.

    MR from John F. Mallard, 30 Nov 60, sub: Conference with Captain Burns W. Spore.

65. Informal transmittal to Ed [Brig. Gen. Edward B. Lansdale, Dep. Asst. to Sec. Def. OSO] from C. Tracy Barnes, 5 Dec 60.

    MR from Thomas A. Parrott, 8 Dec 60, sub: Minutes of Spl. Group Meeting, 8 Dec 60.

66. Cables to Guatemala from Director: 9 Dec 60, DIR 15777 (OUT 51475) and 14 Dec 60, DIR 16285 (OUT 52820); to Director from Guatemala: 11 Dec 60, GUAT 680 (IN 15363) and 14 Dec 60, GUAT 691 (IN 16784).

67. Cable to Director from Guatemala, 15 Dec 60, GUAT 702 (IN 17704).

68. Esterline-Pfeiffer OH Int., *op. cit.*, Tape 1, pp. 10-12.

69. Oral History Interview: Richard D. Drain by Jack B. Pfeiffer, 8 Jan 76, Tape 2B, pp. 50-52.

   Richard D. Drain, Personal Notes, 9 Dec 60.

70. Drain-Pfeiffer OH Int., *op. cit.*

70a. Drain, Personal Notes, 15 Dec 60.

71. Memo for DCI from C. Tracy Barnes, 21 Dec 60, sub: Cable GUAT 702 (IN 17704), dated 15 Dec 60.

72. MR from John F. Mallard, 22 Dec 60, sub: Meeting with DOD Regarding Personnel Support for JMATE. (DD/P 0-6704).

73. Memo for Deputy Asst. to Sec Def for Spl. Ops. from C. Tracy Barnes, 27 Dec 60, sub: Special Force Trainers.

73a. Memo for DDP/CIA from Graves B. Erskine, 3 Jan 61, sub: US Military Personnel Support of Project CROSSPATCH. TS.

74. Memo for Asst. Sec Def OSO from Jacob D. Esterline, 5 Jan 61, sub: Requirement for US Army Spl Forces to Support Project CROSSPATCH.

74a. Memo for the President from Christian A. Herter, 25 Nov 60, sub: Message of November 19, 1960 from the President of Guatemala. U.

74b. Memo for the President from Christian A. Herter, 12 Jan 61, sub: Telegram from Guatemalan President, Miguel Ydigoras Fuentes. U.

74c. Telegram for Amembassy Guatemala from Secretary, 13 Jan 61, Amembassy Guatemala 464. C.

75.   Cables to Bell from Guatemala: 1 Jan 61, GUAT
      805 (IN 1489); 13 Jan 61, GUAT 822 (IN 1699);
      14 Jan 61, GUAT 829 (IN 1808); 15 Jan 61, GUAT
      831 (IN 1883); and to Director, 12 Jan 61, GUAT
      816 (IN 30054).

75a. Office Memo to Chief, WHD from C/WH/4, 11 Jan 61,
      sub: Press Release by Guatemalan Ambassador to
      US.

75b. Official Routing Slip to Chief, WHD from Walter
      Elder, 9 Jan 61, sub: Article from *The Nation*. U.

      New York Times, 10 Jan 61.

      MR from J. C. King, 11 Jan 61, sub: Meeting to
      Discuss Proposed Release to the Press re *NYT*
      Story, etc.

      Extract from *The Nation*, 19 Nov 60.

      Memo for the DCI from Stanley J. Grogan, 9 Dec 60,
      sub: [Transmittal of magazine article for Victor
      Tasky]. U.

      The Nation, 7 Jan 61, pp. 7-9.

      Memo for the DCI from John S. Warner, 10 Jan 61,
      sub: Request of Representative Frank Kowalski
      (D., Conn.). (ER 61-374).

75c. MR from J. C. King, 11 Jan 61, sub: Meeting to
      Discuss Proposed Release to the Press re *NYT*
      Story, etc.

75d. Memo for Chief, WHD from J. D. Esterline, 11 Jan
      61, sub: FRD Fronting for Paramilitary Activities
      in Guatemala.

75e. *Ibid*.

76.   *Washington Post*, 24 Mar 61.

77. E. Howard Hunt, *Give Us This Day* (New Rochelle,
     N.Y., 1973), pp. 113-137.

     Cables: To Bell from MADD, 13 Feb 61, MADD 1498
     (In 4765); to Bell from Guatemala, 15 Feb 61,
     GUAT 974 (IN 4943).

     R. D. Drain, Personal Notes, 20 Feb 61.

78. MR from Jacob D. Esterline, 5 Apr 61, sub: Meet-
     ing with Adolph [*sic*] A. Berle.

     Cable to Bell from Guatemala, 31 Mar 61, GUAT 1200
     (IN 0949).

78a. Cable to Director from Guatemala, 10 Jul 60, GUAT
     903 (IN 22607).

79. MR from Jacob D. Esterline, 24 Feb 61, sub: Meet-
     ing with President Miguel Ydigoras Fuentes, *et al.*

     Cable to Bell from Guatemala, 15 Feb 61, GUAT 974
     (IN 4943).

80. Cables: To Bell from Guatemala, 21 Mar 61, GUAT
     1160 (IN 4224); to GUAT from Bell, 21 Mar 61,
     BELL 3003 (OUT 7693).

80a. *New York Times*, 2 Jan 62.

     Cuba, Ediciones Venceremos, *History of an Aggression*
     (Havana, 1964), pp. 190, 192, 253.

81. Memo for Mr. Ralph A. Dungan from L. D. Battle,
     16 Mar 61, sub: Letter from President Ydigoras of
     Guatemala. TS.

     Cables to Bell from Guatemala: 25 Feb 61, GUAT
     1048 (IN 1014); 27 Feb 61, GUAT 1052 (IN 1230);
     4 Mar 61, GUAT 1094 (IN 2129).

     Cable to Guatemala from Bell, 25 Feb 61, BELL 1993
     (OUT 5131).

82. [MR from Thomas A. Parrott] Minutes of Spl. Group Mtg., 2 Mar 61.

83. NBC White Paper, "Cuba, Bay of Pigs," 1964. U. (CIA Film No. T6134.)

84. Memo of Conversation [from R. A. Godfrey], 22 Mar 61, sub: Guatemalan Foreign Minister's Call on the Secretary. C.

85. MR from Jacob D. Esterline, 5 Apr 61, sub: Meeting with Adolph [*sic*] A. Berle.

86. Cables to Bell from Guatemala: 14 Apr 61, GUAT 1267 (IN 3419); 17 Apr 61, GUAT 1279 (IN 3982); 18 Apr 61, GUAT 1292 (IN 4340); 19 Apr 61, GUAT 129[8?] (IN 4491).

87. *Ibid.*, 19 Apr 61, GUAT 1299 (IN 4492).

88. *Ibid.*, 17 Mar 61, GUAT 1134 (IN 3765).

89. *Ibid.*, 2 May 61, GUAT 1393 (IN 1113).

90. *Ibid.*, 18 May 61, GUAT 1449 (IN 2094); from Bell to Guatemala: 14 May 61, BELL 0550 (OUT 9176); 19 May 61, BELL 0656 (OUT 9370).

91. Memo for Chief, WHD from Jacob D. Esterline, 29 Apr 61, sub: Meeting with Carlos Alejos Arzu, etc.

92.

93. *Ibid.*, p. 1.

Foreign Service List, January 1962. U.

Source References

Part II

Nicaragua

1. Cable from Managua to Director, 14 Jun 60. MANA
   3226 (IN 11800).

2. Dispatch from ⬚ Managua to Chief/WHD, 23 Sep 60,
   sub: JMNET/ ⬚ MR concerning his TDY Managua.
   ⬚ -2357.

3. *Ibid.*

4. *Ibid.*

5. *Ibid.*

6. *Ibid.*

7. *Ibid.*

8. *Ibid.*

9. MR from L. P. Napoli, 11 Oct 60, sub: Trip to
   Nicaragua.

   Memo for Chief, WH/4 from J. Hawkins, 30 Sep 60,
   sub: Survey of Nic Air/Maritime Support and Op
   Sites.

10. MR from L. P. Napoli, 15 Oct 60, sub: Results of
    Nicaraguan Trip.

11. MR from N. Imler, R. W. Brown, and ⬚ ,
    25 Oct 60, sub: Nicaragua Survey Trip -- 13 to
    20 Oct 60.

12. Letter from Wm. (Rip) Robertson to [General C. P.
    Cabell] 26 Aug 60 and subsequent notes, memos,
    etc. pertaining to letter dated 25[?] Aug 60.

13. Memo for Irving G. CADICK (P) from J. C. King, 2 Dec 60, sub: Letter of Instruction.

14. *Ibid.*

15. *Ibid.*

16. Memorandum for Chief/WH/4 from Asst. Ch/DPD, 30 Nov 60, sub: Status of JMTIDE (JMC-0211).

17. Memo for Record from L. P. Napoli, 28 Sep 60, sub: Telephone call to Ambassador Thomas B. Whelan.

18. Memo for Record from Jacob D. Esterline, 24 Oct 60, sub: Meeting with DCI and Assistant Secretary of State for Latin America, Thomas Mann, on Cuba.

    Memo for A/DDP/A from Jacob D. Esterline, 28 Dec 60, sub: JMTIDE.

19. Memo for DDP from C. Tracy Barnes, 18 Nov 60, sub: Points re Cuba for Discussion at Special Group Meeting, Saturday, 19 Nov 60.

20. Memo for DDP from J. C. King, 18 Nov 60, sub: CONUS Military Installations for JMARC Training Sites.

    MR from Richard D. Drain, 21 Nov 60, sub: JMARC Meeting with DDP.

    MR from Richard D. Drain, 22 Nov 60, sub: JMARC Meeting with DDP.

21. Memo To Whom it May Concern [from William Robertson], 30 Nov 60, sub: Questions Robertson Feels Should Be Answered or Discussed Prior to His Departure.

22. Blind Memo as Revised by C/WH and Delivered by [Col. J. F.] Mallard to [Frank] Devine for [Thomas] Mann Evening of 1 Dec [60]. Includes handwritten note [2 Dec 60?] from R[ichard] D. D[rain], Ch/WH/4/P&P.

23. *Ibid.*

24. Memo for the Special Group from [WH/4], 3 Dec 60, sub: Nicaraguan Aspects of Cuban Operation.

    Memo for DDP/EMB from Jacob D. Esterline, 6 Dec 60, sub: Four JMARC Problems for 8 December Meeting of Special Group.

25. Cable from Director to Managua, 5 Dec 60, DIR 14854 (OUT 99557).

26. Dispatch from ____ Managua to Chief/WH, 9 Dec 60, sub: JMNET/JMARC Transmittal of Reports by Irving G. CADICK Regarding JMARC Activities. ____-2410.

27. *Ibid.*

28. *Ibid.*

29. *Ibid.*

30. MR from David R. McLean, 9 Aug 72, sub: Conversation with Louis P. Napoli.

31. *Ibid.*

32. Cables: From Director to Managua, 10 Dec 60, DIR 16028 (OUT 51871); from Managua to Director, 19 Dec 60, MANA 3358 (IN 19007); from Managua to Director, 19 Dec 60, MANA 3359 (IN 19238).

33. Memo from Jacob D. Esterline to A/DDP/A, 28 Dec 60, sub: JMTIDE.

34. Cable from Managua to Director, 19 Dec 60, MANA 3358 (IN 19007).

35. Memo from C. Tracy Barnes for DCI, 2 Jan 61, sub: Material for Policy Meeting on Cuba, 3 Jan 61.

36. *Ibid.*

37. MR from Richard D. Drain, 4 Jan 61, sub: Meeting with A/DDP/A.

38. Memo from C. Tracy Barnes for DCI, 5 Jan 61, Material for the 5 January Special Group Meeting.

39. James Burwell, *Logistics Support for Operations in Cuba, March 1960 - October 1961*, DDS Historical Series, OL-7, April 1971, p. 38.

    Cable from Director to Managua, 21 Dec 60, DIR 17569 (OUT 55338).

40. Memo from J. Hawkins for Chief, WH/4, 4 Jan 61, sub: Policy Decisions Required for Conduct of Strike Operations Against Government of Cuba.

41. Cable from Managua to Bell, 14 Jan 61, MANA 3391 (IN 1797).

42. Memo from J. C. King for DCI, 19 Jan 61, sub: Visit of General [Anastasio] Somoza de Bella [*sic*], Director-General of the Nicaraguan Army.

    MR from L. P. Napoli, 23 Jan 61, sub: Visit of General Somoza with the Director on 21 Jan 61.

43. Memo from Chief, WH/4 for Chief, WHD, 9 Feb 61, sub: DLF $2,000,000 Emergency Loan for Nicaragua.

    Memo from Radford W. Herbert for Chief, WH/4, 10 Feb 61, sub: DLF $2 Million Emergency Loan for Nicaragua.

44. Memo from J. C. King for DCI, 28 Feb 61, sub: Nicaraguan Aspects of Project JMATE. (ER 61-1687 with Transmittal Slip from [ ] 11 May 61 and Official Routing Slip from WH/4/P&P [12 Jun 61?]).

45. *Ibid.*

46. Situation Report, JMTIDE from Irving G. CADICK, 17 Jun 61.

    Contact Report: Three Meetings CADICK/[ ] since 3 Jan 61, 17 Jan 61. U.

47. Situation Report, JMTIDE from Irving G. CADICK, 17 Jan 61. U.

Contact Report: Three Meetings CADICK/⬚ since 3 Jan 61, 17 Jan 61. U.

48. Cable from Managua to Bell, 1 Feb 61, MANA 3428 (IN 3433).

Cable from Bell to Managua, 1 Feb 61, BELL 1071 (OUT 7894).

49. Cable from Bell to Managua, 9 Feb 61, BELL 1370 (OUT 8693).

49a. Memo for Special Plans and Operations Branch, J-5 Division, JCS/DOD from R. K. Davis, 12 Jun 61, sub: Restrictions on Travel of Military Personnel in Nicaragua (DPD 3695-61).

50. Contact Report from William Robertson, 15 Feb 61, sub: 14 February Meeting between President Somoza and William Robertson.

51. *Ibid.*

52. Cable from Managua to Bell, 15 Feb 61, MANA 3445 (IN 4961).

53. Cables from Managua to Bell: 5 Feb 61, MANA 3443 (IN 3901); 14 Feb 61, MANA 3453 (IN 4874); 28 Feb 61, MANA 3479 (IN 1454).

Cable from JMWAVE to Bell, 25 Feb 61, WAVE 3964 (IN 1029).

Letter from R[ichard] D. D[rain] to Jack B. Pfeiffer, 24 Jan 76. U.

54. Cables from Managua to Bell: 17 Feb 61, MANA 3462 (IN 0290); 19 Feb 61, MANA 3465 (IN 0494).

Cables from Director to Managua: 24 Feb 61, DIR 26695 (OUT 76761); 24 Feb 61, DIR 26738 (OUT 76962); 24 Mar 61; DIR 31559 (OUT 87849).

Memo for Record from L. P. Napoli, 15 Mar 61, sub: Conversation between Ambassador Sevilla-Sacasa and Napoli.

55. Cables from Director to Managua: 24 Feb 61,
    DIR 26695 (OUT 76761); 24 Feb 61, DIR 26738
    (OUT 76962).

56. Cable from Managua to Bell, 19 Feb 61, MANA 3465
    (IN 0494).

57. Memo for Record from L. P. Napoli, 15 Mar 61,
    sub: Conversation between Ambassador Sevilla-
    Sacasa and Napoli.

58. Memo from L. P. Napoli [for Gerard Droller],
    27 Mar 61, sub: Principal Officer -- JMATE
    Activities in Nicaragua.

59. *Ibid.*

60. Taylor Committee: MR's of PM Study Group Meetings,
    Conversation with Colonel Hawkins [n.d., presumed
    subsequent to 30 May 61], pp. 5-6.

61. Memo from Capt. B. W. Spore for DDP, 7 Mar 61,
    sub: Utilization of US Military Personnel by
    Project CROSSPATCH.

62. Cable from Managua to Bell, 11 Apr 61, MANA 3561
    (IN 2888).

63. *Ibid.*, 13 April, MANA 3568 (IN 3164).

64. Cable from TIDE to Bell, 13 Apr 61, TIDE 527
    (IN 3230). TS.

65. Dispatch from COB, JMWAVE to Chief, WHD, 31 May 61,
    sub: Operational/JMATE, Mario Guyon Diaz (-1666).

65a. Cable from Managua to Bell, 24 Jan 61, MANA 3415
    (IN 2569).

66. Cable from TIDE to Bell, 15 Apr 61, TIDE 569
    (IN 3486).

66a. Dispatch from COB, JMWAVE to Chief, WHD, 31 Mar 61,
    op. cit.

66b. Cable to TIDE from Director, 25 Apr 61, (No TIDE number) (OUT 7991).

67. Cable from Managua to Bell, 22 Apr 61, MANA 3615 (IN 4968).

68. Dispatch ⬚ -1666, 31 May 61, *op. cit.*

69. Cable from Managua to Bell, 15 Apr 61, MANA 3582 (IN 3518).

70. Cable from Managua to Bell, 15 Apr 61, MANA 3583 (IN 3517).

71. Memo for Record from L. P. Napoli, 4 May 61, sub: Conversation between Ambassadors Whelan and Sevilla-Sacasa.

72. Cable from Managua to Director, 22 Jun 61, MANA 3680 (IN 29002).

OFFICIAL HISTORY

OF THE

BAY OF PIGS OPERATION

VOLUME II

PARTICIPATION IN THE CONDUCT

OF FOREIGN POLICY

(pages 168-255)

Volume II

Participation in the Conduct
of Foreign Policy

Contents

Appendixes

.Appendix 1

Guatemalan Revolt, November 1960:

Miscellaneous Cables

DATE: NOV 13 1845Z 60   EMERGENCY

TO: DIRECTOR   IN 41822

FROM: GUATEMALA CITY

EMERGENCY DIR PACY CITE GUAT 508

REF: GUAT 507 (IN 41125)*

   MIDEF RUBEN GONZALEZ SIGUI URGENTLY REQUESTS ODYOKE

SUPPLY ANY INFO CONCERNING ANY ENEMY SHIPS NOW IN POSITION

ACT AGAINST GUATEMALA.

                        END OF MESSAGE

* Reported attack by unidentified forces against Guatemala City at 0300 local 13 November.

DATE: NOV 13 1850Z 60   EMERGENCY

TO: DIRECTOR   IN 41824

FROM: JMADD

EMERGENCY DIR GUAT CITE MADD 0541

    1. IN VIEW OF LOCAL DISTURBANCES AND RIOTING IN
SURROUNDING TOWNS, STRONGLY RECOMMEND CANCELLATION OF
MISSION GS-46-007.

    2. PREPARED TO DEFEND MADD WITH U.S. AND CUBAN
PERSONNEL. PRESENTLY SUPPORTING GUAT CITY WITH C-46
TRANSPORT OF GUAT TROOPS TO GUAT CITY.

    3. DISBURSED TWO B-26's TO GUAT CITY PER REQUEST
SANTORO.

                    END OF MESSAGE

        SIGNAL CENTER NOTE: THIS MSG HAS BEEN SENT TO DPD.

DATE: NOV 13 2038Z 60

TO: GUATEMALA CITY JMADD JMTRAV

FROM: DIRECTOR

EMERGENCY

OUT 91802

CITE DIR: 11284

EMERGENCY GUAT EMERGENCY MADD TRAV

JMNET

    IF NOT ALREADY DONE PLACE ALL CUBAN PE RSONNEL ON
FULL ALERT AND PREPARE FOR ANY CONTINGENCY. ADVISE ON
CONTINUING BASIS ANY DETERIORATION IN SITUATION.

END OF MESSAGE

Releasing Officer

  C.KING, CHIEF, WHD

Authenticating Officer

  J.D. ESTERLINE, CHIEF, WH/4

DATE: NOV 13 2050Z 60   OPERATIONAL IMMEDIATE

TO: JMADD   OUT 91807

FROM: DIRECTOR

OPIM MADD INFO GUAT KOLA RIMM YOGU CITE DIR 1288

     CANCEL GS-46-007 PLAN TO EFFECT EVACUATION IF

REQUIRED AT DIRECTION OF [ ] SUPPORT [ ] IN INTERIM

AS REQUIRED. CARPENTER DUE TO TAKE OFF FROM KWCANINE

AT 0500L 14 NOV. IF SITUATION WORSENS SEND DELAY OF

MISSION MSG TO EGLI RPT EGLI OTHERWISE AIRCRAFT WILL

PROCEED ACCORDING TO SCHEDULE.

               END OF MESSAGE

Releasing Officer:

    Stanley W. Beerli A/C DPD

Coordinating Officer:

    Mr. Esterline by phone WH/4

FROM: GUATEMALA CITY   Control: 7063

TO: SECRETARY OF STATE   Recd: Nov 13, 1960
                                                  7:50 P.M.
NO: 223, NOVEMBER 13, 3 P.M.

NIACT

PASS ARMY AND AIR FORCE

REFERENCES: EMBTEL 222

   [ZACAPA]
XACAVA/(SECOND MILITARY ZONE HEADQUARTERS) AND PUERTO
BARRIOS MILITARY BASE INCLUDING AIRPORT ARE IN HANDS
UNIDENTIFIED REBELS. PUZZLE IS WHETHER ATTACK ON CUARTEL
GENERAL FAILED OR WAS PLANNED MERELY TO OBTAIN VEHICLES
AND ARMS AND AMMUNITION (WHICH WERE OBTAINED). EMBASSY
OFFICER JUST TELEPHONED FROM BARRIOS SAYING GOVERNOR
IXABEL DEPARTMENT ARRESTED AND MATIAS de GALVEX RADIO
CALLING FOR ANTI-GOVERNMENT REVOLT -- BUT SIGNIFICANT
THAT SO FAR REBEL BROADCASTS MENTION NO NAMES OR PARTY
AFFILIATIONS.

MID-MORNING GAF STRAFED XACAVA AND BARRIOS WITH ROCKETS
AND 50 CALIBRE MACHINE GUNS DESTROYING SEVERAL TRUCKS.
EMBASSY UNDERSTANDS GOG PLANS ATTEMPT RETAKE BARRIOS
BASE AS SOON AS POSSIBLE WITH AIRLIFTED TROOPS FROM GUATE-
MALA CITY PRECEDED BY GAF STRAFING.

YDIGORAS DECLARED STATE OF SIEGE AND CONGRESS MEETING
4 P.M. TO RATIFY IT. (CAS RECEIVING CONFLICTING REPORTS
RE NATURE MOVEMENT.)

EMBASSY IGNORANT WHETHER MOVEMENT CASTROITE OR MERELY
ANTI-GOVERNMENT AND TO WHAT EXTENT ARMY DEFECTIONS IN-
VOLVED. MILITARY GARRISON GUATEMALA CITY AND GAF APPARENTLY
LOYAL AND NO ADVERSE INFORMATION YET FROM REST COUNTRY
OTHER THAN BARRIOS AND XACAVA [ZACAPA].

                                        MUCCIO

Note: Passed Army & Air Force

Ready by Mr. Godfrey (ARA) 8:30 P.M. 11/13 CWO-JSW

DATE: NOV 13 2112Z 60   EMERGENCY

TO: DIRECTOR   IN 41832

FROM: GUATEMALA CITY

EMERG DIR INFO PACY CITE GUAT 511

REF: GUAT 508 (IN 41822)**

    1. AMBASSADOR REQUESTS IMMEDIATE ARRANGEMENTS

BE MADE WITH APPROPRIATE ODYOKE OFFICIALS FOR SURVEIL-

LANCE SOONEST BETWEEN PUERTO BARRIOS AND CUBA, WITH

IMMEDIATE NOTIFICATION [   ] OF RESULTS OF SURVEILLANCE.

    2. ADVISE [   ] ASAP THAT TYPE SURVEILLANCE TO

BE EMPLOYED, WHEN AND WHERE BEING SENT, SO CAN ADVISE GOG

TO ASSURE NO OPPOSITION TO SURVEILLANCE EFFORT BY GUAT

AIR FORCE. CHIEF GAF BEING ADVISED BY EMBASSY OF AMBAS-

SADOR;S REQUEST.

END OF MESSAGE

** Midef Ruben Gonzalez Sigui urgently requested ODYOKE
supply any information concerning any enemy ships now in
position to act against Guatemala.

DATE: 13 Nov 60 [time illegible]   EMERGENCY

TO: GUATEMALA CITY   OUT 91831

FROM: DIRECTOR   CITE DIR: 11293

(OPERATIONAL IMMEDIATE) PACY

RE: GUAT 511 (IN 41822)*

    1.   TWO PLANES (PV-2) [P2V] WILL SURVEILL GULF OF HONDURAS AREA NEAR PUERTO BARRIOS EARLY DAYLIGHT HOURS 14 NOV. WILL CONTINUE PANAMA AND REPEAT SWEEP 15 NOV. SAME HOURS.

    2.   DESTROYER BEING DISPATCHED TO PATROL GULF OF HONDURAS AREA. APPROX ETA ON STATION 15 NOV 60.

END OF MESSAGE

* Guatemala City advised that Mindef Ruben Gongalez Sigui urgently requested ODYOKE to supply any information concerning any enemy ships which were in position to act against Guatemala.

Releasing Officer

Jacob D. Esterline

DATE: NOV 13 2154Z 60   EMERGENCY

TO: DIRECTOR   IN 41833

FROM: GUATEMALA CITY   CITE: GUAT 513

INFO (EMERGENCY) MADD (EMERGENCY) TRAV
SITUATION REPORT
RE A. GUAT 507 (IN 41825)**
   B. GUAT 512*

    1. DUE NECESSITY TO COMMIT LOYAL TROOPS ONLY GUAT
ARMY REQUEST [   ] MOVE ALL GUAT TROOPS FROM FINCA AND
MADD FOR DEPLOYMENT AGAINST REBEL FORCES IN PUERTO BARRIOS-
ZACAPA AREA. MADD C-46'S USED AS TROOP TRANSPORTS.

    2. IN ORDER ASSURE DEFENSE OF MADD ARMING 200 TRAV
CUBANS AND MOVING THEM TO MADD IMMEDIATELY.

    3. LT. COL. EGAN PROCEEDING TRAV AND LT. COL. NEAL
PROCEEDING MADD TO TAKE COMMAND RESPECTIVE BASES. SANTORO
REMAINING WITH [   ] FOR OVERALL COMMAND AND COORDINATION.

    4. GOG HAS REQUESTED USE MADD B-26'S AND PBPRIME
PILOTS VOLUNTEERING FIGHT FOR GUAT IF NECESSARY. REQUEST
HQS IMMEDIATE THINKING RE THIS MATTER.

    5. MAJORITY CUBANS TRAV HAVE VOLUNTEERED TO FIGHT
FOR GUAT AND GOG HAS INDICATED THEY WOULD LIKE USE TRAV
CUBANS AGAINST REBELS IF NECESSARY. REQUEST AUTHORITY
THEIR USE IF NEED ARISES.

                    END OF MESSAGE

* No record in Cable Secretariat as of 1800 13 Nov.
** Reported attack on Guatemala City by unidentified forces.

DATE: NOV 13 2159Z 60   EMERGENCY

TO: DIRECTOR   IN 41835

FROM: MADD   CITE MADD 0542

EMERGENCY DIR INFO EMERGENCY GUAT EGLI

    1.   REQUEST B-26's NOW AT EGLI BE PLACED ON
STANDBY ALERT FOR POSSIBLE USE DEFENSE OF MADD.

    2.   REQUEST ANY AVAILABLE INFO ON AIRCRAFT WHICH
COULD BE USED ON EVACUATION PLANS. AS OF 132030Z MADD
HAS ONE C-46 AT MADD. ALL OTHER AIRCRAFT AT GUAT CITY.
UNABLE TO EVACUATE ALL PERSONNEL [   ] WITH
PRESENT AIRCRAFT SHOULD THIS BECOME NECESSARY. ADVISE.

                   END OF MESSAGE

     THIS MESSAGE WAS RELAYED TO DPD BY SIGNAL CENTER.

DATE: NOV 13 2354Z 60   EMERGENCY

TO: DIRECTOR   IN 41848

FROM: GUATEMALA CITY   CITE: GUAT 512

                                    ┌─────────────────┐
                                    └─────────────────┘
                                       BASED ON: ┌────┐ 1864
                                                 └────┘

DIR PACY

INTEL

SUPDATA SOURCES PARAS 1 AND 2 ┌──────────┐ FROM ┌──────────────┐

OFFICER IN PUERTO BARRIOS; PARA 4 ┌──────────────────┐

┌──────────┐ ; PARA 5 ┌──────────┐ FROM ┌──────────────────┐

┌──────────┐ ; PARA 6 ┌──────┐ PARA 7 ┌──────────┐

FILED: 132130Z

┌──────┐ 1864, GUATEMALA

SUBJ 13 NOV REVOLUTIONARY ATTEMPT AGAINST GUATEMALAN GOVT

DOI: 13 NOV 60 PADA GUATEMALA, GUATEMALA 13 NOV 60 APR

PARAS 1-4 (2); PARAS 5-7 (3)

SOURCES PARAS 1 AND 2 HIGH GUATEMALAN OFFICIALS (B); PARA

3 USIS OFFICER; PARA 4 ┌────────────────────────┐ GUATE-

MALAN ┌──────────────┐ (B); PARA 5 GUATEMALAN JOURNALIST WITH

GOOD POLITICAL CONTACTS (B) FROM RIGHTIST POLITICAL LEADER

(C); PARA 6 RIGHTIST POLITICIAN AND ARMY COL (F); PARA 7

LEFTIST POLITICIAN (F).

Comment: No separate cable distribution is being made
          of this ┌──────┐

CIA INFORMATION REPORT

COUNTRY: GUATEMALA

SUBJECT: REVOLUTIONARY ATTEMPT AGAINST
GUATEMALAN GOVERNMENT

REPORT NO:

DATE OF INFO: 13 NOV 1960

DATE DISTR: 13 NOV 60

PLACE & DATE ACQUIRED: Guatemala, Guatemala City
(13 November 1960)

PRECEDENCE: PRIORITY

REFERENCES: IN 41848

FIELD REPORT NO: 1864

1. EARLY MORNING 13 NOV 60 GUATEMALAN ARMY REBELS
MADE COORDINATED COUP ATTEMPTS AGAINST MARISCAL ZAVALA,
GUARDIA DE HONOR AND MATAMOROS GUATEMALAN ARMY INSTALLA-
TIONS. OWING PROMPT ACTION BY MINISTER DEFENSE RUBEN
GONZALEZ SIGUI, MARISCAL ZAVALA AND GUARDIA DE HONOR
REMAINED IN GOVT HANDS. REBELS TOOK MATAMOROS.

2. UNKNOWN NUMBER GUATEMALAN ARMY TROOPS IN
PUERTO BARRIOS LEFT THE CITY MORNING 13 NOV FOR UNKNOWN
DESTINATION. (SOURCE COMMENT: TROOPS BELIEVED TO HAVE
GONE TO ZACAPA.) NOT KNOWN IF TROOPS HAVE DEFECTED.

3. PUERTO BARRIOS AIRPORT IN HANDS REBELS WAS
STRAFED TWICE BY GUATEMALAN AIR FORCE PLANES. MATIAS

DE GALVEZ RADIO STATION ALSO FELL TO REBELS NOW BROAD-
CASTING ANTI YDIGORAS PROPAGANDA.

4.   ON 13 NOV REBELS TOOK ZACAPA AIRFIELD AND MILI-
TARY BASE. AIR FORCE STRAFED BASE AND AIR FIELD WITH
5-INCH ROCKETS AND 50 CALIBER MACHINE GUNS. ONE PLANE
DAMAGED BY GROUND FIRE. ALL ARMS TAKEN BY REBELS IN
NIGHT ATTACK ON CUARTEL GENERAL.

5.   REBEL FORCES LED BY THREE COLONELS WHO POLITI-
CALLY UNAFFILIATED BUT WHO LEAN TOWARD NON-COMMUNIST LEFT.
PART OF GUATEMALAN AIR FORCE IS COMMITTED TO NEUTRALITY
IN PASSIVE SUPPORT OF COUP. FAR LEFT WILL BE EXCLUDED
FROM COUP BY FORCE IF NECESSARY. COUP WILL REQUIRE 72
HOURS AFTER WHICH COALITION GOVT WILL BE FORMED WITH REP-
RESENTATIVE FROM EACH NON-YDIGORAS PARTY TO INCLUDE PARTIDO
DE UNIDAD REVOLUCIONARIA (PUR).

6.   COUP LEADERS ARE LT. COL. RAFAEL SESAN PEREIIRA,
WHO FOUGHT AGAINST LIBERATION ARMY OF COL. CARLOS CASTILLO
ARMAS; MAJOR JULIO NHINAS, AN OFFICER ON DUTY AT MATAMOROS
DURING COUP; LT. COL. AUGUSTO LOARCA, MILITARY SCHOOL IN-
STRUCTOR. ALL HAVE NON-POLITICAL HISTORY. (SOURCE COMMENT:
POLITICIANS FROM EXTREME LEFT BELIEVED TO BE BEHIND THREE
COUP LEADERS.)

7.

OF PARTIDO REVOLUCIONARIO (PR), SAID CIVILIAN

LEADER OF REBELS IS MANUEL COLON ARGUETA AND THAT PR
SUPPORTS REVOLT.

    8. (FIELD COMMENT: PRESIDENT YDIGORAS DECLARED
30 DAY STATE OF SIEGE. CONGRESS CALLED INTO EMERGENCY
SESSION.)

    9. FIELD DISSEM: STATE, ARMY, AIR, CINCARIB

END OF MESSAGE

DATE: 14 NOV 0001Z 60   EMERGENCY

TO: DIRECTOR   IN 41849

FROM: GUATEMALA CITY

EMERG DIR CITE GUAT 514

     1.   [   ] REQUESTS FOLL ITEMS THROUGH AIRATT:

       A. MINIMUM 200 ANTI-PERSONNEL DEMOLITION
BOMBS 100 LBS. EACH.

       B. 200 SUB-MACHINE GUNS OR BROWNING AUTOMATIC
RIFLES AND AMMO.

     2. AIRATT CANNOT PRODUCE. CAN ABOVE BE SUPPLIED
BLACK THROUGH MADD?

END OF MESSAGE

DATE: NOV 14 0001Z 60   EMERGENCY

TO: DIRECTOR   IN 41850

FROM: GUATAMALA CITY

TO DIR INFO MADD CITE GUAT 515

GOG REQUESTS IF AT ALL POSSIBLE SEND NAPALM
BOMBS TO BE MOUNTED ON GOG B'26'S. DELIVERY TO BE
BLACK TO MADD. PLEASE ADVISE.

END OF MESSAGE

DATE: NOV 14 0044Z 60   EMERGENCY

TO: GUATEMALA CITY   OUT 91823

FROM: DIRECTOR   CITE: DIR 11291

TO EMERGENCY GUAT INFO EMERGENCY MADD TRAV

RE A.   GUAT 514 (IN 41849)*

   B.   GUAT 515 (IN 41850)**

        WORKING ON REF REQUESTS BUT TO DELIVER NEED

YOUR ADVISE SOONEST AS TO AVAILABILITY SECURE AIRFIELDS

PARTICULARLY MADD AND SAN JOSE. ALSO DO YOU HAVE UNLOAD-

ING AND DISTRIBUTION CREWS AND FACILITIES.

                    END OF MESSAGE

* [   ] (1) request for arms and ammunition
   through AIRATT. Latter could not produce. Queried if
   could be supplied black through MADD.

**GOG requested if at all possible send napalm bombs to
   be mounted on GOG B-26's.

Releasing Officer:

   William Bradley by direction of A/CSDO

   C. Tracy Barnes ADDP/A

                    - 184 -

FROM: GUATEMALA

TO: SECRETARY OF STATE

NO: 225, NOVEMBER 14, 1 a.m.

Control: 7268

Recd: Nov 14, 1960
9:50 a.m.

PRIORITY

PASS ARMY AND AIR FORCE

EMBTEL 223

STILL ONLY CONFLICTING REPORTS AS TO NATURE MOVEMENT.

FOREIGN MINISTER VISITED ME IN EXCITED STATE AT 8 P.M. AT
BEHEST PRESIDENT SAYING HOPED US WOULD PREVENT SEA OR AIR-
BORNE INVASION FROM CUBA AND ASSIST IN CASE INVASION FROM
NEIGHBORING COUNTRY. INSISTED UPRISING WAS CASTRO-INSPIRED
AND THAT GOVERNMENT HAS LONG BEEN PREDICTING WOULD HAPPEN.
SAID HE HAD JUST SENT STRONG TELEGRAMS INCRIMINATING CUBA
TO OAS AND UN. ALSO SAID PR AND MARIO MENDEZ MONTENEGRO
WHO LEFT FOR US TWO DAYS AGO HEAVILY INVOLVED. SAID MEN-
DEZ PLANNED RETURN TO ASSUME LEADERSHIP MOVEMENT IF SUCCESS-
FUL.

ACTUAL SITUATION LITTLE CHANGED. GAF HAS BEEN STRAFING
BARRIOS AND ZACAPA ALL DAY AND LATE THIS AFTERNOON AIR-
LIFTED 100 OR SO TROOPS TO CHIQUIMULA TO MOVE AGAINST
ZACAPA TONIGHT OR TOMORROW MORNING. ELEMENTS OF MARISCAL
ZAVALA IS REGIMENT REPORTEDLY ALSO ON WAY TO PORT AREA.
GOVERNMENT PRONOUNCEMENTS HAVE VARIOUSLY BLAMED UPRISING
ON COMMUNISTS (PGT) AND MENDEZ MONTENEGRO.

MUCCIO

Note: Passed OSD, Army, Navy, Air 11/14/60, CWO-JRL.

DATE: NOV 14 0448Z 60   EMERGENCY

TO: DIRECTOR   IN 41880

FROM: GUATEMALA CITY   CITE: GUAT 517

EMERG DIR CITE GUAT 517

    GOG URGENTLY NEEDS AND REQUESTS MINIMUM 100,000
ROUNDS 50 CAL. ARMOUR PIERCING AND TRACER AMMO SOONEST,
BY 14 NOV IF AT ALL POSSIBLE. [   ] HAS DETERMINED
GOG HAS ONLY 15,000 ROUNDS LEFT FOLLOWING 13 NOV ACTION.
AIRATT STATES THAT AT PRESENT RATE USE GOG WILL EXHAUST
PRESENT SUPPLY EARLY 14 NOV. PLEASE ADVISE.

                    END OF MESSAGE

DATE: NOV 14 0613Z 60   EMERGENCY

TO: GUATEMALA CITY   OUT 91833

FROM: DIRECTOR   CITE: DIR 11295

TO GUAT INFO MADD

RE GUAT 517 (IN 41880)*

    1. ARRANGING TRANSPORTATION. WILL ADVISE ETA.

    2. UTILIZE .50 CAL AMMO IF AVAILABLE MADD STOCKS.
ADVISE QUANTITY ON HAND.

END OF MESSAGE

*GOG urgently needs and requests minimum 100,000 rounds
50 cal armour piercing tracer ammo soonest, by 14 Nov
if at all possible.

Releasing Officer:

  J. Esterline

Authentication Officer:

  W. Eisemann

DATE: NOV 14 0636Z 60   OPERATIONAL IMMEDIATE

TO: JMADD   OUT 91835

FROM: DIRECTOR   CITE: DIR 11297

TO MADD RE MADD 0542*(IN 41835)

   1. B-26'S ON STANDBY EGLIN.

   2. EVACUATION PLAN WILL BE AUGMENTED WITH TWO
C-54'S ARRIVING MADD P.M. 14 NOV.

               END OF MESSAGE

`* MADD requested a B-26 at Eglin AFB be placed on standby
alert for possible use in the defense of MADD.

Releasing Officer:

  Stan Beerli

Coordinating Officer:

  J. Esterline

DATE: NOV 14 1016Z 60   EMERGENCY

TO: GUATEMALA, JMADD, JMTRAV   OUT 91920

FROM: DIRECTOR   CITE: DIR 11321

TO GUAT MADD TRAV INFO RIMM YOGU

    1. IN EVENT ANY OR ALL OF ABOVE ADDRESSESS FORCED
CLOSE DOWN DUE ENEMY ACTION AND THERE IS NOT TIME FOR EVEN
SHORT SITUATION REPORT SEND EMERGENCY QUEBEC SIGNAL INDICA-
TING "FORCED TO EVACUATE."

    2. QUEBEC SIGNALS ASSIGNED AS FOLLOWS:

        A. FOR GUAT: QWW *

        B. FOR MADD: QXX

        C. FOR TRAV: QZZ

    3. ABOVE TO BE TRANSMITTED ONLY UPON AUTHORIZATION
SENIOR KUBARK OFFICIAL EXCEPTING AS LAST DITCH PROPOSITION
COMMO OFFICER MAY SEND.

    4. RIMM AND YOGU COVERING ABOVE STATIONS RESPEC-
TIVELY ON 24 HOUR BASIS.

    5. IF EVACUATION BECOMES NECESSARY REQUEST ABOVE
ATTEMPT TAKE RS-1 AND NECESSARY CRYSTALS AND PADS TO PER-
MIT CONTINUED CONTACT WITH RESPECTIVE BASES.

    6. ADVISE HQS ACTION YOU ABLE TAKE INCLUDING ANY
SPECIAL INSTRUCTIONS TO RIMM AND YOGU.

                END OF MESSAGE

Releasing Officer: D/CO
Coordinating Officers: OC-S [   ]; WH/IV Stanulis by phone
Authenticating Officer: W.S.Georgia, Jr.

DATE: NOV 14 1504Z 60   EMERGENCY

TO: DIRECTOR   IN 42027

FROM: JMADD   CITE: MADD 0540

TO (EMERG) DIR INFO (EMERG) GUAT

RE: A. DIR 11294 (OUT 91832)

      B. DIR 11295 (OUT 91833)*

     PER REF A RESOURCES FOR NAPALM BOMB PREPARATION

AND INSTALLATION NOT AVAILABLE. GROUND CREW NOT EXPER-

IENCED IN HANDLING NAPALM BOMBS.

     PER REF B ONLY 15,000 ROUNDS, .50 CAL NEEDED FOR

LOCAL RESERVE AND 16 ROCKETS AVAILABLE AT MADD.

                    END OF MESSAGE

* Stated arranging transportation will advise eta.

DATE: NOV 14 1523Z 60   OPERATIONAL IMMEDIATE

TO: EGLIN AIR FORCE BASE   OUT 91865

FROM: DIRECTOR   CITE: DIR 11303

OPIM EGLI INFO OPIM MADD GUAT

    REQUEST CARPENTER AND KEKOLER PREPARE DEPART

FOR MADD ASAP. LOAD MAX AMOUNT 50 CAL COMMENSURATE

FLYING SAFETY IN BOMBAY PRIOR DEPARTURE. WX DUE EGLI

1700Z. WHEN CARPENTER READY DEPART NOTIFY HQS BY PHONE.

             END OF MESSAGE

Releasing Officer:
   Stanley W. Beerli AC/DPD

DATE: NOV 14 1630Z 60   OUT 91832

TO: GUATEMALA CITY   CITE: DIR 11294

FROM: DIRECTOR

TO GUAT INFO MADD TRAV EGLIN

RE: A.   GUAT 514 (IN 41849)*

      B.   GUAT 515 (IN 41850)**

      1. PER REF A, FOLLOWING BEING PREPARED FOR SHIP-
MENT VIA TWO C-54'S: 200 SMG CAL .45; 100,000 RDS AMMO
CAL .45; AND APPROX 70 BOMBS FRAG 220 LBS.

      2. PER REF B, TECHNICAL PERSONNEL NOT IMMEDIATELY
AVAILABLE FOR NAPALM BOMB PREPARATION AND INSTALLATION.
RECOMMEND MADD MUNITION RESOURCES BE CHECKED AND UTILIZED.

      3. EGLIN: PROVIDE ETA TO MADD AND GUAT. RECALL
PLAN MUST BE INCLUDED AND CREW FULLY BRIEFED. ADVISE HQ
OF PLAN DETAILS.

                              END OF MESSAGE

*   [   ] requested a minimum of 200 anti-personnel
    demolition bombs, 100 lbs each, and 200 sub-machine guns
    or browning automatic rifles and ammo.
** The GOG requested napalm bombs be sent to be mounted on
    GOG B-26's.

Releasing Officer:
  J. Esterline
Coordinating Officers:
  O/L
  DPD - OK per Stan Beerli
Authenticating Officer:
  W.E.Eisemann
                      - 192 -

DATE: NOV 14 2150Z 60   OPERATIONAL IMMEDIATE

TO: EGLIN AIR FORCE BASE   OUT 91993

FROM: DIRECTOR   CITE: DIR 11352

OPIM EGLI MADD GUAT

A.   MSN ES-54-049 AND ES-54-050.

B.   TAKEOFF TIME WILL BE FURNISHED BY HQS VIA ⬜ X.
TWO C-54G AIRCRAFT SHOULD BE LOADED AND PREPARED FOR
TAKEOFF ASAP AFTER C-124 ARRIVAL.

C.   TWO C-54G DELIVER 20,000 LBS MUNITIONS TO MADD.

D.   EGLIN FIELD THREE.

E.   MADD

F.   AUTHORIZED USE OF USAF AND OSTIARY CREWS OR COMBINA-
TIONS.

G.   BOTH AIRCRAFT UNMARKED EXCEPT FOR TAIL NUMBERS 6096
AND 9069. CALL SIGN FOR FIRST AIRCRAFT ES-54-049 IS RASCAL
ONE AND SECOND AIRCRAFT IS RASCAL TWO. COMPLAN FOR
RASCAL ONE IS LIMROT, FOR RASCAL TWO IS PEKSOR.

H.   ROUTE TO GUAT IS DIRECT MERIDA, DIRECT GUAT CITY,
DIRECT MADD. AIRCRAFT CONTACT MADD TOWER ON ARRIVAL
WITH CALL SIGN. AIRCRAFT WILL NOT LAND UNLESS COUNTERSIGN
"RHUBARB" RECEIVED FROM TOWER. IN EVENT TOWER IS OUT
MADD WILL COUNTERSIGN LOW PASS WITH RED FLARE FOLLOWED

BY GREEN FLARE. AMERICAN WILL MAN TOWER. IN EVENT
COUNTERSIGN NOT RECEIVED AIRCRAFT RETURN EGLIN THREE
SAME ROUTE. COMPLAN REPORTING POINTS AS FOLLOWS:

(1)   2600N   8800W

(2)   MERIDA RBN

(3)   1750N   9000W (GUAT BORDER)

(4) GUAT CITY

(5) MADD

EGLI ADVISE HQS, MADD, GUAT, RIMM AND YOGU OF ATD,
ETA AT MADD AND ETA AT CHECKPOINT THREE.

I. ACFT WILL NOT TAKEOFF MADD UNTIL FLIGHT PLAN AND DE-
PARTURE TIME APPROVED HQS AND UNDERSTANDING AND CONCURRENCE
ACKNOWLEDGED BY MADD.

J. FOR MADD: ACKNOWLEDGE UNDERSTANDING AND CONCURRENCE
THIS MSG.

K. FOR GUAT: ADVISE MAJ BATRES ETAS AT GUAT BORDER
(CHECK POINT THREE) UPON RECEIPT TO INSURE NO INTERCEPT.

END OF MESSAGE

Releasing Officer:

  Stanley W. Beerli AC/DPD

Coordinating Officer:

  C/JMCLEAR C/COMMO/DPD

OPIM EGLI MADD GUAT RIMM YOGU

A.   ES-54-049 (LIMROT) AND ES-54-050 (PEKSOR).

B.   MSNS APPROVED.

C.   LIMROT TAKEOFF 15/0700Z.

D.   PEKSOR TAKEOFF 15/0830Z.

E.   WILL ADVISE DEPARTURE DATE AND TIMES FROM MADD.

END OF MESSAGE

Releasing Officer:
  Stanley Beerli AC/DPD

Coordinating Officer:
  C. Barquin for C/JMCLEAR

DATE: NOV 14 2225Z 60   OPERATIONAL IMMEDIATE

TO: EGLIN AIR FORCE BASE   OUT 92018

FROM: DIRECTOR   CITE: DIR 11367

OPIM EGLI

REF A. [   ] -X ES 54-049

    B. [   ] -X ES 54-050

1. PER TELECON VARTANIAN/HAYES FOLL BEING DELIVERED
YOUR ST VIA C-124 FOR TRANSHIPMENT TO JMADD. REQUEST SHIP-
MENT BE FORWARDED ON PRIORITY BASIS CITED.

    A. 50 EA 220 LBS FRAG BOMBS 13,151 LBS 1ST PRIORITY

    B. 16,800 RDS 50 CAL AMMO   6,531 LBS 2nd PRIORITY

    C. 200 EA .45 CAL SMG   4,821 LBS 3rd PRIORITY

    D. 60,000 RDS .45 CAL AMMO   3,530 LBS 4TH PRIORITY

2. PARTIALS OF ITEM PARA 1 A and B ABOVE SHOULD BE
SHIPPED ON EACH ACFT FOR SPACE UTILIZATION AND FOR EACH AIR-
CRAFT NOT TO EXCEED 10,000 LBS OF CARGO.

3. BALANCE OF C-124 SHIPMENT TO BE HELD FOR FUTURE
FLIGHTS.

4. REQUEST HQS BE ADVISED WHAT FACILITIES AVAIL
EGLI FOR STORAGE OF ABOVE TYPE MATERIEL FOR 7-14 DAY PERIODS.

                          END OF MESSAGE

Releasing Officer:
  George Gaines C/JMCLEAR

Coordinating Officers:
  DPD/AS RLS WH/4 [   ] (Telecon)

DATE: NOV 14 2231Z 60   PRIORITY

TO: GUATEMALA   OUT 92070

FROM: DIRECTOR   CITE: DIR 11409

PRIORITY GUAT INFO PRIORITY MADD TRAV

REF: GUAT 513 (IN 41833)*

        HQS CONCURS ASSIGNMENT NEAL AS COB JMADD AND

EGAN AS ACTING COB JMTRAV. PLAN REPLACE EGAN ASAP FOR

RETURN HQS.

                        END OF MESSAGE

*   Lt. Col. Egan proceeding TRAV and Lt. Col. Neal
    proceeding MADD to take command respective bases.

Releasing Officer:
  R. Bissell, DD/P
Coordinating Officers:
  J. Hawkins, C/WH/4/PM
Authenticating Officer:
  J.C.King C/WHD

DATE: NOV 14 2233Z 60   OPERATIONAL IMMEDIATE

TO: RIMM EGLIN AIR FORCE BASE YOGURT   OUT 92024

FROM: DIRECTOR   CITE: DIR 11371

OPIM RIMM EGLI YOGU

     1. TENTATIVE ETD MISSION ES-54-049 (PLAN LIMROT)
15/0700Z, ETA MADD 15/1320Z. CHECK POINTS:

    A. 2600 N 8800 W (TAKE OFF TIME PLUS 1:45)

    B. MERIDA BEACON (TAKE OFF TIME PLUS 3:40)

    C. 1750 N 9000 W (TAKE OFF TIME PLUS 4:50)

    D. GUAT CITY   (TAKE OFF TIME PLUS 5:55)

    E. MADD   (TAKE OFF TIME PLUS 6:20)

    2. TENTATIVE ETD MISSION ES-54-050 (PLAN PEKSOR)
15/0830Z, ETA MADD 15/1450Z. CHECK POINTS SAME AS LIMROT.
FREQUENCIES FOR PEKSOR SAME AS LIMROT.

    3. IF RIMM RECEIVES TRANSMISSION FROM LIMROT AT
CHECK POINT 5 INDICATING THEY ARE DIVERTING TO ALTERNATIVE
BASE OR RETURNING EGLIN, RIMM IS DIRECTED TO PASS SIMILAR
INSTRUCTIONS IMMEDIATELY TO PEKSOR ADVISING QKDAWN AND
EGLIN AFTER ACCOMPLISHING.

    4. FINAL ETD THESE MISSIONS WILL BE FURNISHED VIA
CABLE.

                              END OF MESSAGE

Releasing Officer:
  Charles F. Quinette D/DPD/OPS
Coordinating Officers
  DPD/AS MAJ SKINNER oC/AD

DATE: NOV 14 2314Z 60   OPERATIONAL IMMEDIATE

TO: EGLIN AIR FORCE BASE   OUT 92069

FROM: DIRECTOR   CITE: DIR 11408

OPIM EGLI INFO OPIM MADD GUAT

RE: DIR 11303 (OUT 91865)*

      RELAY CARPENTER DISREGARD REF. PROCEED MADD
15 NOV SAME TIMES ORIGINALLY SCHEDULED 14 NOV WX PERMIT-
TING. TACTICAL CALL SIGN B-26 IS RASCAL THREE. USE
TACTICAL CALL CONTACTING MADD TOWER. MADD TOWER WILL
ANSWER COUNTERSIGN RHUBARB INDICATING SAFE LAND MADD.
EVENT ACFT RADIO FAILURE BUZZ MADD TOWER ONE TIME. MADD
TOWER FIRE ONE RED THEN ONE GREEN FLARE INDICATING SAFE
TO LAND. SAME PROCEDURE APPLIES EVENT MADD TOWER RADIO
FAILURE. SAN JOSE ALTERNATE AIRFIELD.

                END OF MESSAGE

* Requested Carpenter and Kokoler prepare depart for
MADD ASAP.

Releasing Officer:
  Stanley W. Beerli AC/DPD

DATE: NOV 14 2355Z 60   PRIORITY

TO: JMADD, GUATEMALA CITY, JMTRAV   OUT 92135

FROM: DIRECTOR   CITE: DIR 11458

TO PRIORITY/MADD INFO PRIORITY/GUAT/TRAV

REF: DIR 11294 (OUT 91832)*

    TWO C-54 CARGO FLIGHTS DUE 15 NOV. CARRYING 50

FRAG BOMBS, 16,800 RDS 50 CAL. EACH AIRCRAFT LIMITED

10,000 LBS DUE TO OPERATIONAL NECESSITY.

                        END OF MESSAGE

*Alerting Guat of planned two C-54 with ordnance items.

Releasing Officer:
  William E. Eisemann C/WH/4/Support
Coordinating Officers:
  Tele Coord: Maj. Skinner, DPD
  [   ] for C.WH/4/PM
  [   ] for C/WH/4/OPS
Authenticating Officer:
  James S. Burwell WH/4/LOG

DATE: NOV 14 2356Z 60   OPERATIONAL IMMEDIATE

TO: EGLIN AIR FORCE BASE   OUT 92025

FROM: DIRECTOR   CITE: DIR 11372

OPIM EGLI INFO OPIM GUAT MADD [   ] MASH

    1. COVER STORY FOR TWO C-54 A/C AND CREW DEPART-
ING 14 NOV 60 FOR JMADD FOLLOWS:

    A. A/C DEPARTED FROM IMMOKALEE, FLORIDA
DESTINED FOR GUAT CITY.

    B. A/C FURNISHED FULLY LOADED AND FUELED
AT IMMOKALEE BY REPRESENTATIVES OF THE FRD.

    C. CREW HIRED BY THE FRD ON ASK NO QUESTIONS
BASIS.

    2. EVERY ATTEMPT SHOULD BE MADE TO JETTISON CARGO
BEFORE EMERGENCY LANDING IN FRIENDLY THIRD COUNTRY. IN
ANY EVENT CREW SHOULD DISCLAIM KNOWLEDGE OF CONTENTS OF
CARGO.

    3. CREW SHOULD BE GIVEN MR. [   ] AS
EMERGENCY CONTACT IN [   ]. ADDRESS FOUND DIR
08685 (OUT86419)

                END OF MESSAGE

Releasing Officer:
  Stanley W. Beerli SC/DPD

Coordinating Officers:
  JMC/SO S Stembridge
  WH/4 J MULLANE (TELECON)

DATE: NOV 15 0233Z 60   OPERATIONAL IMMEDIATE

TO: DIRECTOR   IN 42405

FROM: MADD   CITE: MADD 0543

OPIM GUAT INFO OPIM DIR

1. REQUEST MEETING WITH [   ]
RE STATUS QUO AT GUAT CITY. CONCERNED OVER TWO C-46'S
WITHOUT CREWS REMAINING AT GUAT CITY MILITARY FIELD.

2. INFO ON SITUATION RELAYED BY FOUR ARMORERS
WHO WERE DETAINED BY OFFICER GROUP AT GUAT CITY FIELD
THIS MORNING AND LATER RELEASED INDICATES GUAT ARMY MAY
ATTEMPT TO SPIKE ALL MILITARY AIRCRAFT TO PREVENT ACTION
BY AIR FORCE. ARMY PERSONNEL ARE POSTED IN ALL GUAT
AF PLANES.

END OF MESSAGE

DATE: NOV 15 [0248?] 60   EMERGENCY

TO: GUAT MADD TRAV   OUT 92236

FROM: DIRECTOR   CITE: DIR 11518

EMERG GUAT MADD TRAV

1.   ODACID REQUESTS FOLLOWING

      A.   SITREP

      B.   CONCRETE PROOF CUBAN INVOLVEMENT SUCH

AS PRISONERS, DOCS, EQUIPMENT.

2.   ANSWER EMERG.   DESIRED BY 15 NOV 1400Z

                    END OF MESSAGE

Releasing Officer:
                    by direction of J.C.King

DATE: NOV 15 1227Z 60   EMERGENCY
TO: DIRECTOR   IN 42628
FROM: GUATEMALA   CITE: GUAT 537

EMERG DIR INFO EMERG MADD TRAV
REFS: A. DIR 11518 (OUT 92236)*
       B. GUAT 521 (IN 42024)**

1. SITREP:
    A. SITUATION AS REPORTED IN REF B STILL APPLIES.
    B. 14 NOV REPORTS OF LEFTIST-COMMUNIST ATTEMPTS
NEGOTIATE REVOLUTIONARY ALLIANCE WITH REBELS TEND TO
SUPPORT REF B PREDICTION THAT POLITICAL GROUPS MIGHT
EXPLOIT SITUATION AND ACTIVELY PARTICIPATE ANTI-GOVT
ACTS.
    C. EXCEPT FOR THE EXPLOSION OF SEVERAL TERRORIST
BOMBS IN STREETS GUAT CITY NIGHT 14 NOV, CALM STILL
REIGNS IN CITY. STATE OF SIEGE WITH CURFEW BEING
ENFORCED.
    D. GUAT ARMY AND AIR FORCE CONTINUING MILITARY
ACTION AGAINST REBELS AND IT STILL TOO EARLY DETERMINE
OUTCOME.
    E. ALTHOUGH ARMY AND AIR FORCE CURRENTLY SUPPORTING
GOG, EVIDENCE EXISTS THAT SOME AIR FORCE OFFICERS ON
VARIOUS LEVELS OBJECT TO SEVERITY OF ACTION BEING TAKEN
AGAINST REBELS. CONTINUED LOYALTY THESE ELEMENTS OPEN
TO QUESTION.
2. NO EVIDENCE CUBAN INVOLVEMENT.
                    END OF MESSAGE

 *ODACID requested concrete proof of Cuban involvement.
**Revolt appeared to be almost purely military with little
  or no political or civilian participation.

DATE: NOV 15 1509Z 60   PRIORITY

TO: DIRECTOR   IN 42700

FROM: JMADD   CITE: MADD 0546

PRIORITY DIR INFO PRIORITY GUAT

1. REQUEST IMMEDIATE DELIVERY AMMO RESUPPLY AS FOLLOW
    A. CARTRIDGES, CAL .30, LINKED, BALL 50,000
    B. CARTRIDGES, CAL .30, IN 8 RND CLIPS 75,000
    C. CARTRIDGES, CAL .30, CARBINE, BALL 10,000
    D. CARTRIDGES, CAL .30, BALL, FOR BAR 10,000
    E. MAGAZINES FOR BAR 50 EA
    F. MAGAZINES FOR CARBINE 100 EA
    G. MAGAZINES FOR THOMPSON SMG 50 EA
    H. PISTOL, AUTOMATIC, CAL .45   24 EA
    I. BELT, PISTOL   24 EA
    J. CLIPS, FOR .45 CAL PISTOL   48 EA
    K. CLIP CARRYING CASE FOR .45 PISTOL   24 EA
2. FIRST THREE ITEMS MOST CRITICAL
3. TOTAL WEIGHT ABOUT 15,200 lbs. CUT ITEM D. FIRST
IF NECESSARY.

                        END OF MESSAGE

DATE: DEC 15 1559Z 60   PRIORITY

TO: DIRECTOR   IN 17634

FROM: GUATEMALA CITY   CITE: GUAT 700

REFS: A. GUAT 655 (IN 12474)*
        B. GUAT 693 (IN 17002)**
        C. GUAT 699 (IN 17440)***

1. IN 13 DEC 60 MEETING WITH [_____], [_____] MADE IT
VERY CLEAR THAT NEW GOVT (RESULTING FROM REVOLT BY MIL GROUP
AND PR-MLN-DCG COALITION) WILL CONTINUE SUPPORT ODYOKE
ANTI-CASTRO OPERATIONS.

2. WHEN [_____] POINTED OUT THAT YDIGORAS FALL WOULD
HELP CASTRO, [_____] EMPHASIZED THAT BOTH MIL AND CIVILIANS
INVOLVED ARE STRONGLY ANTI-COMMUNIST AND ANTI-CASTRO AND
WOULD BE EVEN MORE FORCEFUL THAN YDIGORAS IN THAT RESPECT.
HE RECOMMENDED THAT ODYOKE GIVE MORAL SUPPORT NOW TO PLOT-
TING GROUP BECAUSE YDIGORAS SURE TO FALL SOON.

3. ALTHOUGH AT OUR REQUEST [_____] HAS IN PAST SUCCESS-
FULLY PREVENTED PR ACTION AGAINST YDIGORAS, HE NOW SAYS
HE CAN NOT STOP COALITION AND CERTAINLY NOT MILITARY AND
NEITHER HE NOR ANYONE ELSE CAN DO ANYTHING TO PREVENT
YDIGORAS OVERTHROW.

                        END OF MESSAGE

  *Sitrep giving [_____] view that another military
   revolt against Ydigoras could take place in the near
   future.
  **Request GALBOND (1) check with ODACID regarding aid
    grant to GOG.
  ***Report on Guatemalan revolutionary activities.

FROM: GUATEMALA CITY   Control: 8173

TO: SECRETARY OF STATE   Recd: Nov 15, 1960
                                                2:56 p.m.
NO: 230, November 15, noon

PRIORITY

EMBTEL 226

GOVERNMENT FORCES HAVE RETAKEN SECOND MILITARY ZONE HEAD-
QUARTERS AT ZACAPA AND RE-ESTABLISHED COMMUNICATIONS WITH
THE CAPITAL. GOVERNMENT PLANS SEND ADDITIONAL TROOPS TO
SECURE ZACAPA PERMITTING OTHERS PUSH ON TO BARRIOS.

SEVERAL BOMBS WENT OFF GUATEMALA CITY LAST NIGHT CAUSING
NO LOSS LIFE BUT SEVERELY DAMAGING MINISTER ECONOMY'S
AUTOMOBILE FRONT HIS HOUSE. CAS HAS REPORTS COMMUNISTS
WILL ATTEMPT STAGE DEMONSTRATIONS PLAZUELA BARRIOS THIS
AFTERNOON.

                              MUCCIO

DATE: NOV 15 1816Z 60   OPERATIONAL IMMEDIATE

TO: DIRECTOR   IN 42807

FROM: JMADD   CITE: MADD 0549

1. REQUEST ONE C-54 REMAIN MADD FOR POSSIBLE
EVACUATION. OTHER C-54 TO RETURN EGLI FOR LOAD.

2. AS SOON AS ONE RETURNS MADD. WILL SEND OTHER
BACK TO EGLI.

3. PROPOSE CONTINUAL SHUTTLE RUN AS ABOVE UNTIL
EMERGENCY IS RESOLVED.

                    END OF MESSAGE

NOTE: This message has been sent to DPD

DATE: NOV 15 1858Z 60   EMERGENCY

TO: DIRECTOR   IN 42828

FROM: GUATEMALA   CITE: GUAT 541

EMERG DIR INFO EMERG MADD

REF: GUAT 540 (IN 42829)

    1. REQUEST ASSIGNMENT TWO ADDITIONAL FULLY

OPERATIONAL B-26 TO JMADD ASAP.

    2. TWO MADD B-26'S BEING TURNED OVER GUAT AIR

FORCE 15 NOV DUE FACT MAJORITY GUAT B-26'S NOT OPERATIONAL

AFTER TWO DAYS COMBAT FLYING.

END OF MESSAGE

DATE: NOV 15 1901Z 60   EMERGENCY
TO: DIRECTOR   IN 42829
FROM: GUATEMALA   CITE: GUAT 540

EMERG DIR INFO EMERG MADD
REF: DIR 11343 (OUT 91978)*

    1. ON 14 NOV [   ] ADVISED IT NECESSARY
GUAT AIR FORCE RECEIVE ADDITIONAL AMMO AND USE OF THE TWO
MADD B-26'S. SITUATION CONSIDERED CRITICAL AS ARMY PUR-
SUING REBELS AND ESSENTIAL IT HAVE AIR SUPPORT. GOG B-26'S
SHOT UP AND NEED MAINTENANCE.

    2. AIR ATTACHE CONFIRMED 15 NOV THAT GOG B-26'S
SHOT UP AND SHOULD NOT BE PUT INTO AIR IN PRESENT CON-
DITION.

    3. AMBASSADOR CONCURS WITH [   ] THAT ABOVE NEED
EXISTS AND [   ] SHOULD BE FURNISHED THIS SUPPORT.

    4. MORNING 15 NOV [   ] REPRESENTING [   ]
PROCEEDED TO MADD TO OBTAIN AMMO AND B-26'S.

    5. [   ] REQUESTED [   ] HAVE GUAT PILOTS TALK
WITH INSTRUCTOR TO MAKE CERTAIN THEY UNDERSTAND AND
QUALIFIED OPERATE AIRCRAFT.

    6. IN REF TO AMMO [   ] AGREED WITH [   ] THAT
BULK TO BE STORED AT MADD AND GUAT CITY BASE SUPPLIED
ON DAY-TO-DAY BASIS.

                      END OF MESSAGE

* Joint ODACID/KUBARK message concerning assistance to GOG.

DATE: NOV 15 1904Z 60

TO: TRAV

FROM: DIRECTOR

OPERATIONAL IMMEDIATE

OUT 92431

CITE: DIR 11564

TO OPIM TRAV INFO MADD, GUAT

    1. ZRMEDRICK SMALL ARMS AND BASIC LOAD AT MADD
INCLUDE 66 PISTOLS, 212 RIFLES, 66 SMG'S, 18 LMG'S, 18
BAR'S, 7 EA. 3.5" ROCKET LAUNCHERS, 4 EA. 57MM RECOILLESS
RIFLES, 6 EA 60MM MORTARS, 18 DEMOLITION KITS, 4 INCENDIARY
KITS, 288 GRENADES, 24 AN/PRC-10'S WITH EXTRA BATTERIES,
40 AT MINES, AND 4 CORPSMAN KITS. COMPASSES, BINOCULARS
AND FIRST AID KITS PACKED WITH WEAPONS.

    2. FIVE-DAY AMMO RESUPPLY THESE WEAPONS AND TRAV
WEAPONS BEING SHIPPED MADD ASAP. ETA FOLLOWS. ALSO SHIP-
PING MEDICAL FIELD SET WITH PLASMA.

END OF MESSAGE

Releasing Officer:
  J.C.KING, C/WHD by
Coordinating Officers:
           , WH/4/OPS
  J. Hawkins, C/WH/4/PM
  W.Eisemann, C/WH/4/SPT
Authenticating Officer:
  W. Eisemann. C/WH/4/SPT

DATE: NOV 15 2120Z 60   OPERATIONAL IMMEDIATE

TO: MADD   OUT 92476

FROM: DIRECTOR   CITE: DIR 11582

OPIM MADD INFO OPIM GUAT EGLI

REF: MADD 0549 (IN 42807)*

   1. RETURN BOTH ACFT TO EGLI.

   2. EXPECT THIRD C-54 IN COMMISSION 17 NOV. WILL
SEND TWO DOWN NIGHT OF 17 NOV. THEN ONE CAN BE RETAINED
PER REF WITH ONE ALWAYS REMAINING AT YOUR [   ]

END OF MESSAGE

* Requested one C-54 remain MADD for possible evacuation.

Releasing Officer:
  Stanley W. Beerli, AC/DPD

- 212 -

DATE: NOV 15 2214Z 60   OPERATIONAL IMMEDIATE

TO: EGLIN AIR FORCE BASE   OUT 92497

FROM: DIRECTOR   CITE: DIR 11592

OPIM EGLI INFO PRIORITY MADD GUAT

HBJADE-X:

    1. EX-54-052 (RASCAL 2)

    2. ACFT 764 WILL REMAIN MADD AFTER CARGO OFF

LOAD. CREW WILL RETURN WITH RASCAL 1.

    3. EXPECT 764 TO RETURN EGLI AFTER DELIVERY 577.

MISSION OF 764 IS PROVIDE EVAC CAPABILITY. EGLI INSURE

CANVAS ROLL-UP SEATS AND SAFETY BELTS INSTALLED PRIOR

DEPARTURE 17 NOV.

END OF MESSAGE

Releasing Officer
  Stanley W. Beerli, AC/DPD

Coordinating Officer:
  C. Barquin, C/JMCLEAR

DATE: NOV 15 2352Z 60   OPERATIONAL IMMEDIATE

TO: GUATEMALA CITY   OUT 92593

FROM: DIRECTOR   CITE: DIR 11667

        REQUEST IMMEDIATE REPORT SITUATION AT PUERTO

BARRIOS WHICH ACCORDING RADIO NEWS REPORTS STILL IN

HANDS REBEL FORCE.

                            END OF MESSAGE

Releasing Officer:
  J.C.King, Chief, WHD

Authenticating Officer:
  J.D.Esterline, Chief, WH/4

PRIORITY

TO: GUATEMALA, JMADD, JMTRAV

OUT 92605

FROM: DIRECTOR

CITE: DIRE 11679

TO PRIORITY/GUAT INFO PRIORITY/MADD, PRIORITY TRAV

REF: A. DIR 11294 (OUT 91832)*
       B. TRAV 0114 (IN 39199)**
       C. TRAV 0108 (IN 36520)***
       D. GUAT 517   (IN 41880)****
       E. GUAT 451   (IN 36927)*****

1. HQ HAS READY FOR SHIPMENT APPROX 151,025 LBS CARGO
AS FOLLOWS:

     A. 20 FRAG BOMBS, REF A, 5200 LBS

     B. 83,200 RDS 50 CAL REF D, 32,000 LBS

     C. 200 SMG and 100,000 RDS AMMO REF A, 11400 LBS

     D. BLASTING CAPS AND TRAINING AMMO REF B, 1600 LBS

     E. EVACUATION RATIONS REF C, 24,000 LBS

     F. FIVE 81 MM MORTORS AND 250 RDS AMMO FOR WEAPONS
PACK AT MADD, 13,775 LBS

     G. FIVE DAY RESUPPLY SMALL ARMS AMMO FOR MADD
WEAPONS PACKS, 50,000 LBS

     H. 50 CAL MG AND AMMO REF E, 3050 LBS

     I. 52 FIVE IN. ROCKETS JMCLEAR TRAINING 10,000 LBS

2. DUE CRITICAL SHORTAGE AIR TRANSPORTATION FACILITIES
REQUEST YOU ADVISE IMMEDIATELY ORDER OF PRIORITY FOR
ABOVE SHIPMENTS.

(page 1 of 2)

3. FYI: 50 CAL AMMO AND FRAG GRENADES SHIPPED VIA
2 C-54 ON 15 NOV NOT INCLUDED IN ABOVE.

END OF MESSAGE

   *ETA two C-54's
  **Request for blasting caps, ammo and hand grenades
 ***Request for evacuation canned goods
****Request for 50 cal ammo
*****Request for anti-aircraft 50 cal guns and mounts

Releasing Officer:
Ed Stanulis, Chief, WH/4/OPS

Coordinating Officers:
  Tele Coord - Vartanian, DPD
  [   ], WH/4/PM
  E.Stanulis, C/WH/4/Ops
Authenticating Officer:
  R.W.Brown, Chief, WH/4/Log

FROM: GUATEMALA CITY

TO: SECRETARY OF STATE

NO. 237, November 15, 6 p.m.

PRIORITY

Dept. Telegram 332.

SOME INFORMATION IN RESPONSE DEPARTMENT TELEGRAM CONTAINED
EMBASSY TELEGRAM 226. THERE IS ALMOST NO EVIDENCE, SHOWING
CUBAN INVOLVEMENT IN CURRENT UPRISING IN GUATEMALA, REPORTS
CONTINUE TO CIRCULATE, HOWEVER, THAT THIS IS THE CASE AND
GOVERNMENT SEEMS CONVINCED THIS IS SO. FOR EXAMPLE, ARMY
ATTACHE JUST APPRISED BY ARMY CHIEF STAFF OF MESSAGE RE-
CEIVED BY DEFENSE MINISTER FROM MILITARY COMMANDER POPTUN
BASE, TRANSMITTING WHAT BASE COMMANDER SAID WAS INTERCEPTED
MESSAGE FROM RADIO CUBANA, PRESUMABLY TO REBEL FORCES AT
BARRIOS, ASKING WHETHER AIRPORT AT BARRIOS USEABLE AND IN-
DICATING PROMISED SUPPLIES WOULD BE FORTHCOMING.

CHIEF OF IMMIGRATION ARTURO AGUIRRE MATHEU TOLD EMBASSY
TODAY THAT ABOUT 10 DAYS AGO, FOLLOWING A VIST TO HONDU-
RAS, HE TURNED OVER TO PRESIDENT INFORMATION SECURED IN
HONDURAS IMPLICATING CAPTAIN ARTURO CHUR DEL CID IN CASTRO
ACTIVITIES HONDURAS, CHUR DEL CID IS REPORTEDLY ONE OF
LEADERS REVOLT WHO LED INITIAL ATTACK NOVEMBER 13 ON CUARTEL
GENERAL (EMBTEL 222). AGUIRRE ALSO TOLD EMBASSY THAT COL.
PAZ TEJADA, CLOSE ASSOCIATE OF ARBENZ AND EXTREME LEFTIST
REVOLUTIONARY, WAS THE MILITARY LEADER BEHIND THE REVOLT.
COLONEL ENRIQUE PERALTA, MINISTER OF AGRICULTURE, TOLD

(contd)

EMBASSY OFFICER YESTERDAY PAZ HAS RECEIVED UNCONFIRMED
REPORTS TO EFFECT PAZ TEJADA RECEIVING MONEY FROM CUBA
FOR HIS REVOLUTIONARY ACTIVITIES.   NEWSPAPERMAN TOLD
EMBASSY OFFICER SOME WEEKS AGO HE "KNEW" PAZ TEJADA HAD
MADE A TRIP TO CUBA SEEKING FUNDS.

<u>IN SUMMATION NEITHER THE EMBASSY NOR CAS SO FAR HAS BEEN
ABLE TO DEVELOP POSITIVE PROOF OF CASTRO INVOLVEMENT IN
THE CURRENT UPRISING.</u>

MUCCIO

DATE: NOV 16 0243Z 60   OPERATIONAL IMMEDIATE

TO   DIRECTOR   IN 43052

FROM: GUATEMALA CITY   CITE: GUAT 545

OPIM DIR INFO OPIM MADD OPIM TRAV

    1. AT 1500/2300Z [ ] REPORTED THAT PUERTO
BARRIOS AND GULLAN [GUALAN] WERE THE ONLY TWO TOWNS
REMAINING IN THE HANDS OF REBELS. HE ADMITS THAT POCKETS
OF RESISTANCE ARE PRESENT BETWEEN THESE TWO TOWNS. HE
FURTHER REPORTED THAT THE AIR FORCE IS SUCCESSFULLY INTER-
DICTING THE HIGHWAY AND RAILWAY BETWEEN THE TWO TOWNS
DURING DAYLIGHT HOURS.

    2. HE FURTHER REPORTED THAT [ ] DEPARTED
FOR PERSONAL INSPECTION OF THE ZACAPA AREA IN MIDDLE OF
AFTERNOON 15 NOV. SMALL SCALE MOPPING UP EXERCISES STILL
GOING ON IN VICINITY ZACAPA. HOWEVER TOWN REPORTED IN
HANDS OF GOVT TROOPS.

END OF MESSAGE

FROM: GUATEMALA CITY   CONTROL: 8996

TO: SECRETARY OF STATE   RECD: Nov 16, 1960
                                                 3:05 p.m.
NO.   238, November 16, 11 a.m.

PRIORITY

EMBTELS 226 and 230.

PRESS, RADIO AND TV 9 p.m. LAST NIGHT REPORTED ON VISIT
TO ZACAPA "BATTLE FRONT". SAID GOVERNMENT FORCES ROUTED
REBELS AND COMPLETELY IN CONTROL THERE. DECLARED GROUND
ACTION AGAINST BARRIOS (AIR OFFENSIVE AGAINST BASE HAS
BEEN CONTINUOUS) WOULD BEGIN TODAY. (WITH ARMING OF CIVIL-
IANS AND CONSOLIDATION REBEL POSITION, THIS COULD BE BLOODY.)
SAID GOVERNMENT WAS INFORMED REBELS HAD RECEIVED AIR FROM
FIDEL CASTRO, THAT "WE ARE ALONE BECAUSE ONLY THE GOVERN-
MENT HONDURAS OF DR. RAMON VILLEDA MORALES HAS OFFERED
ITS HELP AND SUPPORT", AND THAT GUATEMALA HAS SATISFAC-
TION NOT A SINGLE FOREIGN SOLDIER AMONG ITS TROOPS. DE-
CLARED COMMUNISTS TRYING EXPLOIT SITUATION AND ENCOURAGED
POPULACE HAVE FAITH AND BE VIGILANT AGAINST COWARDLY STREET
BOMBING ACTIVITIES, ET CETERA.

STREET DEMONSTRATIONS CALLED FOR LAST EVENING QUITE UN-
SUCCESSFUL. ESTIMATED 100-200 PERSONS APPEARED, SOME OF
THEM CRYING "DOWN WITH YDIGORAS" AND "VIVA CASTRO". BUT
WERE QUICKLY DISPERSED BY POLICE WITHOUT UNTOWARD INCIDENT.

UNDERSTOOD CASUALTIES AMONG GOVERNMENT TROOPS ZACAPA
ABOUT 50 KILLED AND NUMEROUS WOUNDED. SOME REBELS TAKEN
PRISONERS BUT MANY FLED TO RESIST ELSEWHERE OR TO TRY JOIN
BARRIOS FORCES. GOVERNMENT FORCES HAVE ARRIVED BARRIOS.

EMBASSY AND CAS HEARING NUMEROUS REPORTS TO EFFECT DISSAT-
ISFACTION WITH YDIGORAS GROWING AND THAT COMMUNISTS ACTIVE
AND VARIOUS OTHER GROUPS ITCHING ACT.

                              MUCCIO

FROM: GUATEMALA CITY   Control: 9180

TO: SECRETARY OF STATE   Recd: Nov 16, 1960
                                               10:53 p.m.
NO.   239, November 16, 5 p.m.
SENT DEPARTMENT 239, REPEATED INFORMATION
    TEGUCIGALPA PRIORITY 10

RELIABLY REPORTED GOVERNMENT TROOPS IN CONTROL BARRIOS
AND COMMUNICATIONS RESUMED WITH CAPITAL. AFTER FAILURE
TO OBTAIN FAVORABLE TERMS SURRENDER, UNDERSTOOD REBEL
LEADERS FLEEING TOWARD HONDURAS. UNDERSTAND ALL AMERI_CANS
SAFE.

                                    MUCCIO

DATE: NOV 16 2329Z 60   PRIORITY

TO: GUATEMALA CITY MANAGUA   OUT 93074
        [   ]
                                         CITE: DIR 11884
FROM: DIRECTOR

PRIORITY GUAT MANA [   ] [   ]

REF: DEPTEL 329*(NOT SENT [   ]

        1. HQS URGENTLY NEEDS DOCUMENTARY EVIDENCE CUBA
BACKING ENEMIES OF REGIME OR DIRECT INVOLVEMENT GOC IN
PLANNING REVOLUTIONARY MOVES FOR FUTURE. IS ANY PROOF
SUITABLE FOR EXPLOITATION AVAILABLE YOUR AREA?

        2. DO YOU SEE ANY OPPORTUNITY TO FABRICATE HARD
EVIDENCE OF GOC PARTICIPATION YOUR AREA?

        3. DOES GOVT HAVE CAPABILITY TO EFFECT QUICK
ROUNDUP OF KNOWN ENEMY ACTIVISTS ON SUITABLE PRETEXT
AND HOLD EVEN 24 HOURS WHILE LODGINGS ARE SEARCHED?

        4. ARE ANY CUBAN CITIZENS CURRENTLY HELD IN JAIL?
IF SO WHO AND ON WHAT COUNTS?

        5. WHAT CUBAN INSTALLATIONS EXIST IN YOUR AREA
WHICH MIGHT BE EXPOSED AS REVOLUTIONARY BASES?

        6. PLS ADVISE ASAP. HQS DESIRES ACCUMULATE USE-
ABLE EVIDENCE SOV-CUBA INSTIGATION AND DIRECTION UPRISINGS
YOUR AREAS.

                        END OF MESSAGE

*OCR/CB notified of reference.

Releasing Officer
    [   ] for J.C.King, Chief, WHD
Coordinating Officers:
  P.E.Oberst, C/WH/CA
Authenticating Officer:
  E.A.Stanulis for J.D.Esterline, Chief, WH/4

DATE: NOV 16 2330Z 60   PRIORITY
TO: JMASH   OUT 93076
FROM: DIRECTOR   CITE: DIR 11886

PRIORITY MASH INFO PRIORITY GUAT
       TRAV, MADD
REF: MASH 1617 (IN 41745)*

1. IN VIEW UNSETTLED CONDITIONS GUAT AND SATURA-
TION TRAV FACILITIES DESIRE MASH SUSPEnD RECRUITMENT OF
PM GROUND TRAINEES UNTIL FURTHER NOTICE. GROUND TRAINEES
ALREADY RECRUITED SHOULD BE RELEASED TO ON CALL STATUS
READY FOR RECALL ON SHORT NOTICE AND MOVEMENT TO TRAV OR
OTHER CAMP AS DIRECTED.

3. FOR TRAV: IF DECISION REACHED TO SEND ADDI-
TIONAL RECRUITS TRAV YOU WILL BE NOTIFIED IN ADVANCE
TO CONSTRUCT ADDITIONAL BARRACKS. PERSONNEL WILL NOT
BE SENT UNTIL YOU INDICATE READY TO RECEIVE.

                    END OF MESSAGE

*MASH has 50-75 PM trainees available shipment TRAV
 within 10 days. Request estimate when shipments to
 TRAV to begin again.

Releasing Officer:
[   ] for J.C.King, C/WHD
Coordinating Officers
[   ] C/WH/4/Support
 J.Hawkins, C/WH/4/PM
Authenticating Officer:
 EAStanulis,C/WH/4

DATE: NOV 17 0036Z 60   OPERATIONAL IMMEDIATE

TO: MADD GUATEMALA CITY   OUT 93064

FROM: DIRECTOR   CITE: DIR 11880

OPIM MADD GUAT INFO PRITY EGLI

REF: MADD 0562 (IN 43622)

1.   ODUNIT HAS REQUESTED NO B-26 AIRCRAFT RETURN
EGLI EXCEPT LAST RESORT.   RETURN BLEHAR AND GREENE VIA
C-54.   DO NOT RETURN ANY B-26 UNLESS PRIOR APPROVAL
RECEIVED.

2.   FOR GUAT: ABOVE ODUNIT POLICY REQUIRES RE-
OPENING WITH [   ] SUBJECT FLYING MADD B-26 AIRCRAFT
COSTA RICA FOR HEAVY MAINTENANCE.   AIRCRAFT TO BE OSTEN-
SIBLE GUAT VEHICLES.   [   ] MAY WISH RECONSIDER
ORIGINAL REFUSAL VIEW SUPPORT HE NOW RECEIVING.

                    END OF MESSAGE

Releasing Officer:
  Stanley W. Beerli, AC/DPD

Coordinating Officers:
  Mr. Esterline (Telecon) WH/4

DATE: NOV 17 2021Z 60   OPERATIONAL IMMEDIATE

TO: GUATEMALA CITY   OUT 93106

FROM: DIRECTOR   CITE: DIR 11909

OPERATIONAL IMMEDIATE GUAT

REF: GUAT 546 (IN 43126)*

 1. TO REMOVE ANY DOUBT THESE ARE CURRENT INSTRUC-
TIONS: CUBAN TROOPS, AIR AND GROUND, ARE NOT TO BE
COMMITTED TO SUPPORT YDIGORAS GOVERNMENT. THIS DOES NOT
MEAN THEY SHOULD NOT DEFEND THEMSELVES IF ATTACKED. BY
SAME TOKEN IF EVACUATION BECOMES A NECESSITY, THEY ARE
AUTHORIZED TO FIGHT THEIR WAY TO EVACUATION POINT.

 2. IF REF SHOULD BECOME A REALITY, NEW INSTRUC-
TIONS WILL BE FORTHCOMING.

END OF MESSAGE

* Base Cmdr at Poptun reported intercept of broadcast
 from Radio Cubana re help forthcoming soon for rebels
 at Puerto Barrios.

Releasing Officer:
 Richard M. Bissell Jr.
Authenticating Officer:
 J.C.King, C/WHD

DATE: NOV 17 2242Z 60   OPERATIONAL IMMEDIATE

TO: GUATEMALA   OUT 93500

FROM: DIRECTOR   CITE: DIR 12092

OPIM GUAT INFO OPIM MADD

    1.   HQS ADVISES ALL KUBARK ACFT SHOULD BE RETURNED
MADD ORDER AFFORD BETTER PHYSICAL SECURITY FLEXIBILITY
AND MAINTENANCE PROVIDED IN REINGRUBER OPINION WILL NOT
PREJUDICE POSITION ☐.   GOG SUPPORT TO BE CON-
DUCTED FROM MADD.

    2.   FOR MADD: REQUEST FUTURE ☐ REPORTS
INDICATE ACTIVITY EACH ACFT ENGAGED IN.   EXAMPLE: GOG,
TNG, FERRY, ETC.

    3.   FOR GUAT AND MADD: ALL MILITARY DETAILEES
AND ANG PERSONNEL ASSIGNED MADD WILL NOT REPEAT NOT
LEAVE PERIMETER LIMITS MADD UNTIL APPROVAL OBTAINED HQS.

                    END OF MESSAGE

Releasing Officer:
  Stanley W. Beerli AC/DPD

Coordinating Officer:
  Mr. Stanulis (Telecon) WH/4

- 226 -

FROM: GUATEMALA CITY

TO: SECRETARY OF STATE

NO: 248, NOVEMBER 18, 5 p.m.

PRIORITY

EMBASSY TELEGRAM 239 AND PREVIOUS.

CONTROL: 10774

RECD: NOV 19, 1960
2:32 p.m.

REBELLION APPARENTLY COMPLETELY DOMINATED, ALTHOUGH SOME
REBELS WITH ARMS AT LARGE IN COUNTRY AND OTHERS FLED TO
HONDURAS. SEVERAL DAYS AERIAL BOMBARDMENT CAUSED REBELS
FLEE BARRIOS. PRESIDENT ARRIVED BY AIR LATE AFTERNOON
NOVEMBER 16 WITH OCCUPYING TROOPS. YDIGORAS RETURNED
TRIUMPHALLY YESTERDAY AND ADDRESSED LARGE WELCOMING CROWD
AT AIRPORT DECLARING INTER ALIA GOVERNMENT VICTORY WARNING
TO COMMUNISTS LEAVE COUNTRY OR BE EXPELLED. LAST NIGHT
YDIGORAS ATTENDED FOOTBALL GAME WITHOUT INCIDENT AND CUR-
FEW MOVED BACK TO 10 p.m.

PRINCIPAL EVENING NEWSPAPER, EL IMPARCIAL, SUSPENDED FOR
20 DAYS UNDER ARTICLE 14 LAW PUBLIC ORDER FOR ARTICLE BY
LIMON BLANCO (HE HAPPENED TO BE CAUGHT IN BARRIOS BY
REBELLION) DISPARAGING NAVY AND AIR FORCE ACTION. TIME
STRINGER ROSENHOUSE YESTERDAY AFTERNOON ON CHARGE HAD
PASSED UNCENSORED INFORMATION ABROAD. INFORMAL CENSOR-
SHIP APPARENTLY BEING EXERCISED AT TELEGRAPH OFFICE.

POLICE ANNOUNCED WOULD SEEN INDICTMENTS AS ACCOMPLICES
REBELLION ALL ARRESTED FOR PARTICIPATION IN DEMONSTRA-
TIONS, UNAUTHORIZED MEETINGS, DISTRIBUTION SUBVERSIVE
PROPAGANDA AND ACTS TERRORISM. SPORADIC LOCAL BOMBINGS
CONTINUING GUATEMALA CITY. NUMBER OF LEFTISTS AND RADI-
CALS ARRESTED INCLUDING EDGAR IBARRA, PRESIDENT LEFTIST
STUDENT ORGANIZATION FUEGO.

EMBASSY HAS STILL SEEN NO EVIDENCE CASTRO INSTIGATION OR
SUPPORT REBELLION. CAS HAD REPORTS, HOWEVER, COMMUNISTS
TRIED JOIN MOVEMENT AFTER IT STARTED BUT REBUFFED BY
REBEL MILITARY. ALSO IT GENERALLY BELIEVED MARIO RENE
CHAVEZ GARCIA, MEMBER PUR AND KNOWN COMMUNIST, WAS IN
BARRIOS DURING REBELLION. PRENSA LIBRE REPORTER CALLED
HIM "CIVIL CHIEF" BARRIOS OPERATION AND SAID HE DIRECTED
PUBLIC MEETING BARRIOS MONDAY NIGHT AT WHICH GOVERNMENT
WAS DENOUNCED AND VICTORY REBEL FORCES PREDICTED. THERE
WAS ABORTIVE MOVE BY EXTREME LEFTIST DEPUTIES TO HAVE
CONGRESS DECLARE YDIGORAS INCOMPETENT TO RULE.

JUST PRIOR SUCCESSFUL QUELLING REVOLT, EMBASSY HEARD
NUMEROUS REPORTS OF PLOTTING AND INDICATIONS FAIRLY WIDE-
SPREAD FEELING YDIGORAS'S DAYS NUMBERED. EMBASSY HAS
IMPRESSION, HOWEVER, YDIGORAS'S POSITION MAY NOW BE
STRONGER THAN BEFORE. HE GAINED PERSONAL PRESTIGE FROM
QUICK VICTORY AND PERSONAL DIRECTION OF OPERATIONS.
LEFTISTS AND DISPARATE RIGHTISTS HAVE SEEN EVIDENCE
HE COURAGEOUS. HE APPEARED COMPLETELY CONFIDENT THIS
MORNING WHEN I TOOK SENATORS HICKENLOOPER AND BUSH TO
SEE HIM. HE TOLD US OF HIS RELENTLESS EFFORTS ESTABLISH
DEMOCRACY IN GUATEMALA, CITING DIFFICULTIES DOING SO IN
VIEW AUTHORITARIAN TRADITIONS AND POINTING EXAMPLES
PROGRESS THIS FIELD SINCE TOOK OFFICE. HE EMPHASIZED
HIS GRAVE CONCERN TODAY NOT MILITARY OR POLITICAL BUT
ECONOMIC.

MUCCIO

DATE: NOV 25 2337Z 60   PRIORITY

TO: GUATEMALA CITY, JMTRAV   OUT 96343

FROM: DIRECTOR   CITE: DIR 13413

PRIORITY GUAT INFO TRAV

REF: A.   GUAT 575 (IN 44738)*
        B.   DIR 12520 (94390 Out)**

1. HQS. DECISION NO KUBARK FLUTTER TEAMS TO PAR-
TICIPATE IN INTERROGATION OF REBEL TYPES CITED REF A.

2. SUGGEST AS ALTERNATIVE GUAT GOVERNMENT ENGAGE
SERVICE OF PBPRIME COMMERCIAL FIRM THIS PURPOSE. HQS.
WILL RENDER APPROPRIATE ASSISTANCE. ADVISE.

END OF MESSAGE

* Request assignment of FLUTTER team for interrogation
   captured rebels GUAT.
** Response to request from GUAT for FLUTTER Team.

Releasing Officer:
  E.A.Stanulis for J.D.Esterline C/WH/4
Coordinating Officers:
  [   ] (by phone), OS/IRD
  J. Langan, C/WH/4/SEC
Authenticating Officer:
  Wm. E. Eisemann, C/WH/4/Support

Appendix 2

Memorandums re Special Force Trainers

A. Four Memorandums of Agreement

B. Memorandum for Chief, WH/4 from
      A/DDP/A, 28 Dec 60

C. Memorandum for Chief, WH/4 from
      A/DDP/A, 30 Dec 60

D. Memorandum for Deputy Assistant
      to the SecDef for Spl Ops,
      30 Dec 60.

MEMORANDUM OF AGREEMENT

It is the purpose of this document to record certain agreements between CIA and President Miguel Ydigoras Fuentes, pursuant to the latter's request to be furnished a U.S. Army military training group to train selected elements of the Guatemalan Army. In furtherance of this purpose, it is agreed as follows:

1. The group will be transported securely by CIA to that area of Guatemala where it will for a period of about eight weeks conduct training of selected individuals in paramilitary activities.

2. It is stipulated that all financial indebtedness incurred hereunder by this group, including payments for salaries, allowances, medical care, food, lodging, equipment, injuries or death and any other support incident thereto, will be borne by CIA.

3. It is agreed that Guatemala will, in the event of necessity, assist in providing medical support, a means of evacuation of this group, and any other support considered necessary for its safety and security, at the expense of CIA.

4. In addition, members of the group are to be allowed entry by means of a secure method which would, as far as practicable, preclude local knowledge of their participation in this area of activity, their safety and protection being the essence of this document. Should any inquiries be directed to official sources in Guatemala regarding the subject personnel, such inquiries will be answered to the effect that they are invitees of the government and are training troops to defend Guatemala against any threat of invasion.

5. This document, which is in keeping with U.S. policy, is entered into for the purpose of maintaining peace and order in the Western Hemisphere and in order to prevent the expansion of Communism therein.

6. It is agreed that this document will remain undisclosed unless both parties agree and will be retained in the custody of the United States. It shall be made available to President Ydigoras at his request.

7. The list of names of the persons comprising the cadre is attached hereto as Annex A.

This agreement is executed this _____ day of _____ 1960.

For the CIA _____   Miguel Ydigoras Fuentes _____

It is the purpose of this document to record certain agreements between CIA and the Republic of Guatemala, pursuant to the latter's request to be furnished a U. S. Army military training group to train selected elements of the Guatemalan Army. In furtherance of this purpose, it is agreed as follows:

1. The group will be transported securely by CIA to that area of Guatemala where it will for a period of about eight weeks conduct training of selected individuals in paramilitary activities.

2. It is stipulated that all financial indebtedness incurred hereunder by this group, including payments for salaries, allowances, medical care, food, lodging, equipment, injuries or death and any other support incident thereto, will be borne by CIA.

3. It is agreed that Guatemala will, in the event of necessity, assist in providing medical support, a means of evacuation of this group, and any other support considered necessary for its safety and security, at the expense of CIA.

4. In addition, members of the group are to be allowed entry by means of a secure method which would, as far as practicable, preclude local knowledge of their participation in this area of activity, since their safety and protection are the essence of this document, which seeks to prevent any unauthorized knowledge of the activity here proposed. Should any inquiries be directed to official sources in Guatemala regarding the subject personnel, such inquiries will be answered to the effect that they are invitees of the government and are training troops to defend Guatemala against any external threat of invasion.

5. This document, which is in keeping with U. S. policy, is entered into for the purpose of maintaining peace and order in the Western Hemisphere and in order to prevent the expansion of Communism therein.

6. It is agreed that this agreement will remain undisclosed unless both parties agree to the contrary and that this document will be retained in the custody of the United States. The document, however, shall be made available to the Republic of Guatemala at its request.

7. The list of names of the persons comprising the cadre is attached hereto as Annex A.

This agreement is executed this _____ day of _____ 1960.

Republic of Guatemala:

By _____   By _____
_____   _____
                                     Ambassador to the United States

- 232 -

MEMORANDUM OF AGREEMENT

It is the purpose of this document to record certain agreements between CIA and
The Republic of ...
President Miguel Ydigoras Fuentes, pursuant to the latter's request to be furnished a
U.S. Army military training group to train selected elements of the Guatemalan Army. In
furtherance of this purpose, it is agreed as follows:

1. The group will be transported securely by CIA to that area of Guatemala where
it will for a period of about eight weeks conduct training of selected individuals in
paramilitary activities.

2. It is stipulated that all financial indebtedness incurred hereunder by this group,
including payments for salaries, allowances, medical care, food, lodging, equipment, injuries
or death and any other support incident thereto, will be borne by CIA.

3. It is agreed that Guatemala will, in the event of necessity, assist in providing
medical support, a means of evacuation of this group, and any other support considered
necessary for its safety and security, at the expense of CIA.

4. In addition, members of the group are to be allowed entry by means of a secure
method which would, as far as practicable, preclude local knowledge of their participation in
this area of activity, since their safety and protection are the essence of this document; it
seeks to prevent any unauthorized knowledge of the activity here proposed. Should any
inquiries be directed to official sources in Guatemala regarding the subject personnel, such
inquiries will be answered to the effect that they are invitees of the government and are
training troops to defend Guatemala against any external threat of invasion.

5. This document, which is in keeping with U.S. policy, is entered into for the
purpose of maintaining peace and order in the Western Hemisphere and in order to prevent
the expansion of Communism therein.

6. It is agreed that this agreement will remain undisclosed unless both parties agree
to the contrary and that this document will be retained in the custody of the United States.
The document, however, shall be made available to *The Republic of Guatemala at its* President Ydigoras at his request.

7. The list of names of the persons comprising the cadre is attached hereto as
Annex A.

This agreement is executed this _____ day of _____ 1960.

_____   by _____
for the CIA   Miguel Ydigoras Fuentes
Tracy ... Barnes

Sterilized copy given [ ]   *Mon 19 Dec at ...,*
+ tried out in Amb. at lunch. [ ] *kept it.*

MEMORANDUM OF AGREEMENT

It is the purpose of this document to record certain agreements between CIA and the Republic of Guatemala, pursuant to the latter's request to be furnished a U. S. Army military training group to train selected elements of the Guatemalan Army. In furtherance of this purpose, it is agreed as follows:

1. The group will be transported securely by CIA to that area of Guatemala where it will for a period of about eight weeks conduct training of selected individuals in paramilitary activities.

2. It is stipulated that all financial indebtedness incurred hereunder by this group, including payments for salaries, allowances, medical care, food, lodging, equipment, injuries or death and any other support incident thereto, will be borne by CIA.

3. It is agreed that Guatemala will, in the event of necessity, assist in providing medical support, a means of evacuation of this group, and any other support considered necessary for its safety and security, at the expense of CIA.

4. In addition, members of the group are to be allowed entry by means of a secure method which would, as far as practicable, preclude local knowledge of their participation in this area of activity. since their safety and protection are the essence of this document, which seeks to prevent any unauthorized knowledge of the activity here proposed. Should any inquiries be directed to official sources in Guatemala regarding the subject personnel, such inquiries will be answered to the effect that they are invitees of the government and are training troops to defend Guatemala against any external threat of invasion.

5. This document, which is in keeping with U. S. policy, is entered into for the purpose of maintaining peace and order in the Western Hemisphere and in order to prevent the expansion of Communism therein.

6. It is agreed that this agreement will remain undisclosed unless both parties agree to the contrary and that this document will be retained in the custody of the United States. The document, however, shall be made available to the Republic of Guatemala at its request.

7. The list of names of the persons comprising the cadre is attached hereto as Annex A.

This agreement is executed this _____ day of _December_ 1960.

Republic of Guatemala:

By __/s/ _____   By __/s/_____
        for the CIA   Carlos Alejos Arzu
                                   Ambassador to the United States

Memo For: Chief, WH/4   28 Dec. '60

From   : A/DDP/A

Subject :   Special Force Trainers

1. Attached is (a) Memo to Lansdale w/draft Memo for Record;
(b) copy of Lansdale's memo on his talk with Douglas approving
the draft Memo for Record; and (c) memo to Mann transmitting
the draft Memo for Record.* Also attached is the original Memo
for Record which is now to be signed by the Guatemalan Ambassador.

2. If it would be of any help to you at all, I would be de-
lighted to go along with you to see the Guat Ambassador. I am
not asking to do this only offering. At any rate, if, as,
and when you are successful with him, I think that I should pick
up the strings with Defense as I have essentially been the ball
carrier there on this problem.

* We received phone call on Tuesday, 28 December advising that
   both Mann and Merchant had approved the draft memo for the
   record.

27 December 1960

MEMORANDUM FOR: Deputy Assistant to the Secretary of
                 Defense for Special Operations

SUBJECT: Special Force Trainers

1.   Following our meeting of December 22 with Assistant
Secretary Irwin, we met on December 23 with Assistant
Secretary Mann.   Mann was extremely hesitant to agree to
any signature by a representative of the State Department to
a document.   After considerable discussion, however, he
did agree to the possibility of having a Memorandum for the
Record prepared (suggested draft attached) which could be
signed by the Guatemalan Ambassador as an accurate statement of the understanding reached between the Government
of Guatemala and the United States.   The Department then
could refer this signed memorandum to the Department of
Defense for appropriate action.

2.   I believe that this arrangement if it could be carried
out would meet the points raised by Mr. Irwin.   Mr. Mann
felt that he would at least have to obtain the concurrence of
Mr. Merchant and possibly of the Secretary.   Before asking
him to do this, it is of course important that we know
definitely whether or not the above proposal would satisfy
the DOD if carried out.   Of course, we have no assurance
at the moment as to whether or not the Guatemalan Ambassador
will be willing to agree.

                              C. TRACY BARNES

Attachment: Proposed Draft

MEMORANDUM FOR THE RECORD

The United States, pursuant to the request of the Government of Guatemala, has agreed to furnish in the near future for an estimated period of three to four months, a U.S. military group to provide specialized training in Guatemala to selected elements of the Guatemalan forces.

The details of this agreement, *and* the procedures whereby it shall be carried out are to be worked out by appropriate representatives of the United States Department of Defense and of the Government of Guatemala.

- -

The above accurately states the understanding reached between the Government of Guatemala and the United States.

_____   _____
(date)   (Signature)

27 December 1960

MEMORANDUM FOR CAPTAIN SPORE

SUBJECT: Agreement with Guatemala

This afternoon, Deputy Secretary Douglas and I discussed the legal basis for introduction of U. S. military personnel into Guatemala for training "CROSSPATCH" personnel. I showed him the memo from Tracy Barnes, subject "Special Force Trainers," dated 27 December, and its attached "Memorandum for the Record" to be signed by the Guatemalan Ambassador to Washington. Also, I told him of the previous document and Assistant Secretary Irwin's objections to it.

After a thoughtful pause, Mr. Douglas said that this "Memorandum for Record" would be acceptable to Defense. He then asked what the next step was. I said that I would inform CIA, who would then handle through State according to Barnes' memo to me. When this memorandum was received by Defense, it would be best if Mr. Douglas held a meeting with Service representatives and told them that this was Defense policy. Mr. Douglas agreed to this suggestion.

After leaving Secretary Douglas, I told Tracy Barnes that Douglas believed the memorandum was acceptable. I asked if he needed a note on this, but he said that my verbal word was sufficient. He said that he would then try to get both State and the Guatemalan Ambassador to approve. I suggested that State's transmittal be addressed to the Secretary of Defense, but be delivered to OSO who would then get it to Secretary Douglas. Barnes said he would have the signed documents hand-carried to OSO for action by Defense.

Note: When the signed documents are received by OSO, Deputy Secretary Douglas should be informed. OSO should promptly arrange a meeting for Mr. Douglas with the Service representatives, so that he can tell them at first-hand that this is policy. Suggest that the number of representatives be kept to a minimum so that it doesn't become a big mob in his office on this very sensitive subject. If John Irwin is in town, he should be included.

If, for some reason, such a meeting cannot be held promptly, then a memo for the Services should be sent to them, signed by Mr. Douglas.

EDWARD G. LANSDALE
Brigadier General, USAF

27 December 1960

MEMORANDUM FOR: Assistant Secretary of State
                for Inter-American Affairs

SUBJECT: Special Force Trainers

1. Attached is a copy of the proposed Memorandum for the
Record" for submission to the Guatemalan Ambassador in
connection with the Special Force Trainers discussed in your
office on Friday, 23 December. If, as it is hoped, the Guatemalan Ambassador will sign the statement in the lower left
hand corner of the attached draft, the document can then be
"sent" from the Department of State to the Secretary of Defense
for appropriate action. This internal U.S. document should, I
think, be handled by only your office and ours although the
receiving office in Defense, i.e. General Lansdale's office,
would be informed.

2. The attached document and the above procedure have
been examined and approved by Deputy Secretary of Defense
Douglas and he has advised us that he will see to it that the
Special Force Trainers are released in accordance with our
request as soon as all steps have been completed.

3. I would appreciate it, therefore, if you could give me
your reaction as soon as possible (by telephone) so that we may
take appropriate steps to obtain the signature of the Guatemalan
Ambassador. I assume that you would prefer to have us do this
in view of the fact that we had the previous dealings with him.
We propose to ask him for this second signature on the grounds
that a document of this type will provide him and his Government
with more secure and sounder protection than the first document.

                                   G. TRACY BARNES

Attachment: Memorandum for the Record

MEMORANDUM FOR THE RECORD

The United States Government, pursuant to the request of the
Government of Guatemala, has agreed to furnish in the near
future for an estimated period of three to four months, a U.S.
military group to provide specialized training in Guatemala to
selected elements of the Guatemalan forces.

The details of this agreement and the procedures whereby it
shall be carried out are to be worked out by appropriate representatives of the United States Department of Defense and of the
Government of Guatemala.

- -

The above accurately states the
understanding reached between
the Government of Guatemala and
the Government of the United States.

signed by Miguel Ydigoras
      (Signature)

29 Dec. '60
      (Date)

Chief, WH/4   30 December 1960

A/DDP/A

Special Force Trainers

    Attached are the latest documents in connection with the Special Force Trainers. One is a memo to Frank Devine attaching a suggested draft letter of transmittal to the Defense Department covering the signed Memo for the Record. The second is a memo to Lansdale transmitting the two original signed agreements.

30 December 1960

MEMORANDUM FOR: Deputy Assistant to the Secretary of
Defense for Special Operations

SUBJECT: Special Force Trainers

1. Attached are the original signed documents in connection
with the Special Force Trainers with which you are familiar.
The first is the agreement, dated 21 December, signed by
both Alejos, the Guatemalan Ambassador to the United States,
and by Jake Esterline; and the second is a Memorandum for
the Record signed by Alejos on 29 December. The latter
document is identical to the one shown to Secretary Douglas
by General Lansdale a few days ago.

2. The State Department will provide (I hope today) the
letter of transmittal covering the Memorandum for the Record
and discussed with General Lansdale. Since, as you know,
we are very anxious to take action as soon as possible, I
hope that you will be willing to act on the attached documents
without waiting for receipt of the letter of transmittal from
the Department of State. As you know, both Assistant Secretary
Mann and Secretary Merchant approved the procedure so there
is not the slightest doubt that such a letter will be provided.

3. I assume that when these documents have served their
purpose, you will either hold them in your files or, if you
prefer, return them to me and I will file them here. Anything
that you can do to expedite this matter will be very much
appreciated. In this connection, in order to keep me up-to-
date, would you be good enough to give me a call when the
matter is under way.

C. TRACY BARNES

Attachments:
1. Agreement dtd 21 Dec.
2. Memo for Record dtd 29 Dec.

Appendix 3

Portion of

Oral History Interview

with

Ambassador John J. Muccio

13 April 1971

Appendix 3

Portion of

Oral History Interview

with

Ambassador John J. Muccio

13 April 1971

Washington, D. C.

by William W. Moss

for the John F. Kennedy Library*

MOSS: Ambassador Muccio, you were ambassador to
          Guatemala beginning in late 1959, if my in-
          formation is correct. The sources that I
          have indicate that the Eisenhower administra-
          tion went ahead with funding of a project to
          invade, or to do something about recapturing,
          Cuba in March of 1960. The money went towards
          training guerrilla bands in Guatemala. I was
          wondering what the first knowledge you had of
          this was. How did it come to your attention,
          in what way, under what circumstances?

MUCCIO: When the liaison to Ydigoras man arrived in
          Guatemala he had a note to me from one of
          the Assistant Secretaries of State saying
          that so and so will approach you on a program
          we intend to be inaugurated in Guatemala.**

---

*   Pages 1-6.

** One such note to Muccio in Guatemala City from R. R.
Rubottom, Jr., Assistant Secretary of State for Inter-
American Affairs, 15 Jul 60, read as follows: "Dear
Much[?] I have asked Bob Davis [Robert K. Davis, ⬚
⬚ who will bring this letter to you, to convey
some information which is very closely held." (Source:
State, FADRC, Micro card file: 60-242, Geneva 762
(3-16-62)-Interior Dept (7-10-62), Operations. S.)

MOSS: All right. Were the terms of that program
          made known to you at that time?

MUCCIO: No.

MOSS: All right. In what way did you begin to
          discover what was going on?

MUCCIO: Well, there were two sources of information
          that were available to me. I received nothing
          official out of Washington, but the liaison
          man had been my CAS (Covert American Source)
          chief for several months before being pulled
          out, and he and his replacement didn't get
          on too well.* But the former liaison man was
          more or less of a compulsive talker and he
          felt freer to talk to me than elsewhere ...

MOSS: In what terms did he put it?

MUCCIO: ... and in that way he brought to my attention
          a lot of developments as they occurred, in
          implementing and carrying out the program.

MOSS: All right. Did he discuss the program itself
          with you, or merely the logistic steps, the
          business of taking over the plantation [Alejos's
          finca], and so on?

MUCCIO: I doubt whether he knew, except what was going
          on in Guatemala, very much of the overall
          strategy.

MOSS: Yes, all right. Now you say you doubt that
          he knew the particulars, or the purpose of
          what he was doing at that time.

---

* This might be a reference to [   ] between
[   ] who was [   ] December 1960 when
[   ]. However, [   ]
remained until after the Bay of Pigs and as noted in
Part I, p. 97 footnote, [   ] was [   ] for the
Cuban ops and [   ] was [   ]
activity.

MUCCIO: As far as he was concerned this was a training
            project. As to whether it was going to be
            used, where and when it would be used, was
            very nebulous to him.*

MOSS: Right. When did you begin to see the thing
            build up and change character? I assume that
            in the early days it looked rather like a
            gerrilla warfare school, much as the Panama
            school is. I wonder at what point you began
            to sense that this was a major development,
            and in what ways.

MUCCIO: Anyone that knew anything about President
            (Miguel) Ydigoras (Fuentes) would know that
            he couldn't keep anything to himself. Ydigoras
            assumed that I knew what was going on and he
            talked. Almost every time I saw him he brough
            out some new fact of what was underway.

MOSS: Yes. Now let me ask this. As I understand
            it, the story broke in the American papers
            after -- what is it? -- *La Hora* in Guatemala
            picked it up.** It broke in the American
            papers around October, just before the elec-
            tion; and then was picked up again by a chap
            named (Paul P.) Kennedy, curiously enough, for
            the *New York Times* in January, and Kennedy
            was expelled from the country over this, as
            I understand, and then brought back. What was
            your involvement in this little episode?

MUCCIO: Practically none. Ydigoras invited me up to
            the two *fincas* where the training was under-
            way, repeatedly, and I repeatedly avoided
            going up there. I never did go up there,
            except on one occasion. That was when, after

---

   * Apparently Muccio's CIA source was not such a "com-
pulsive talker" as Muccio had indicated or else the
source was not [   ] -- [   ] was fully aware of
the operational plan.

** Presumably this is a reference to the use of
Guatemalan sites for training the Cubans.

it had become a matter of conjecture in the
American press and media, Ydigoras invited
the whole diplomatic corps up there for an
asado, with a sleight of hand he had all the
Cubans run up to the other *finca*, and brought
in some of the Guatemalans who were being
trained at the same time. He took all of us
around and said, "See, everybody's saying that
there's been Cubans here; there's nothing
but Guatemalans. My boys are being trained."*

MOSS: Did anybody swallow this?

MUCCIO: Dam[n] few. (Laughter) You must remember
         that most of those Cuban youngsters were from
         the so-called better classes. They had means,
         and they ran all over that country.

         There were these specially marked jeeps, or
         unmarked jeeps, going in all directions at
         all times. I'm sure that more were killed
         on the roads of Guatemala than were killed
         at the Bay of Pigs.

MOSS: The whole ineptitude of the operation is
         amazing, not only what you're talking about
         now, but I was struck by the simple tactics
         at the beach. It was just incredible to me
         that it could have been done that way, but
         that's an aside -- my opinion.

MUCCIO: On that point let me mention that I under-
         stand the same chief of operations handled
         the Bay of Pigs preparation, implementation,
         or whatever term you want to use, that had
         handled the famous Guatemalan incident.

---

* The Agency cable traffic does not reflect any such
outing for the diplomatic corps. US newsmen and
members of the Congress of Guatemala were given such
escorted tours.

MOSS: Oh, yes.

MUCCIO: When -- what was his name -- (Jacobo) Arbenz ...

MOSS: Yes. In 1954.

MUCCIO: ... 1954, was left isolated and CIA (Central Intelligence Agency) supported Castillo Armas, who came in from Honduras. I doubt whether a single shot was fired by one or the other side in the march from Honduras into Guatemala City. Guatemalan military are brought up in a school where no officer, no member of the armed force ever points a gun at another member, another individual in uniform, period. And I'm afraid some of the haphazard planning was due to the ease of the Guatemalan ...

MOSS: I see.

MUCCIO: ... incident in 1954. They were not aware of the control that (Fidel) Castro had already established in Cuba.

MOSS: Yes, Yes, I understand. Now in March of 1961, after the new administration took over, Roberto Alejos went to Washington with a letter from Ydigoras.

MUCCIO: Go ahead.

MOSS: Yes. I was going to say, had you foreknowledge of this, and were you aware that Ydigoras was trying to put pressure on the Americans to get this thing moving.

MUCCIO: Well, on two occasions the liaison officer came to me and said that they were having trouble keeping the boys under control; that they'd been trained to such a pitch that they were eager to get this thing going. He wanted to know if I wouldn't write to Washington saying that it was time to use these excellently prepared (laughter) ...

MOSS: Yes. And what was your response to this?

MUCCIO: My response was that I had not been consulted
           in any way, and I had no role to play in that
           particular phase of this operation.

MOSS: Were you informed before the Alejos trip that
           he was going?

MUCCIO: No. I know that Alejos had been going back
           and forth.

MOSS: When did you first receive official word of
           what was going on from the department?

MUCCIO: That was before anything really was underway,
           when the liaison man came down to establish
           his role there in Guatemala. His role was
           merely liaison between the operating group
           and President Ydigoras. Roberto Alejos was
           right in the midst of this.

MOSS: Now did you have any specific instructions
           from the State Department on this?

MUCCIO: Not any.

MOSS: Okay, now let me ask you when the operation
           was underway, when it became apparent that
           it was going to end in disaster, what was
           the reaction of Ydigoras, of Alejos and
           other Guatemalans to this, and of the CIA
           people who were in Guatemala at that time?

MUCCIO: Well ... None of the CIA men responsible
           for that operation ever came anywhere near
           the Embasssy. They were always up in the
           ... They had their own transportation, their
           own communication facilities and everything

else. I took the position that I had not personally seen anything going on, which was the reason why I dismissed Ydigoras' repeated invitations to go up and see how fine the boys were doing. I could legitimately say I had not seen them myself. That was very help-ful, particularly when it became a public issue.*

MOSS: Yes. Do you recall how Ydigoras responded to the failure of the invasion? Do you recall his mood, his attitude?

MUCCIO: Well, his whole attitude was that some of the people in Washington were scared of their own shadow.

MOSS: How about your CAS liaison man? Was he still there after it went off?

MUCCIO: For a while, yes.

MOSS: Do you recall his reaction?

MUCCIO: Well, that something had gone wrong.

MOSS: Nothing specific?

MUCCIO: He was there for a while because the question as to what to do with all this equipment that had been brought down there came up. Now I had a role to play in that.

MOSS: All right. Let me shift the topic somewhat. Well, let me ask you first ... I would be negligent if I didn't ask you about your personal feeling about the operation: its wisdom, its implementation, and so on, with hindsight of course, and realizing that this is one man's perspective. Would you comment in general on it?

---

* [   ] in the American Embassy.

MUCCIO: Well, I had good grounds to be very skeptical of Ydiogras. He was a man who preferred to be mischievous, even when it was not to his advantage. They were not under CIA or the US. These were his boys. He talked about them incessantly every time I saw him. He talked loosely about this to many others. His lack of perception and sensitivity was evident in the baffling attempt to use Cubans to suppress the revolt of his army on November 13, 1960. I heard of his plan to inject Cubans into this purely Guatemalan fray as follows:

Midnight, Saturday, November 13, a third of the Guatemalan armed forces "took off" against Ydigoras. At La Aurora Air Force headquarters, junior officers disarmed and isolated the Chief of Staff. Shortly thereafter some had misgivings, could not agree on the next move and decided to let the Americans know what was underway, particularly since they had received word that Ydigoras had secretly ordered some DC-3 planes loaded with Cubans flown to Puerto Barrios where the revolt was most active.

They'd first called in Lieutenant Colonel (William J.) Cavoli, who was the air attache. Cavoli didn't know what to do and called Colonel John Berry, senior Army attache. Just as soon as Berry arrived there and saw what was underway he called my deputy (Robert F.) Bob Corrigan. Bob Corrigan said, "this is something the ambassador should know about right away." The whole American group came up to the embassy residence. The liaison man came in a few minutes later and said that the Cuban trainees were already airlifted and should have landed by now in Puerto Barrios. I turned around to the liaison man -- he had instant access to Ydiogoras at all times -- and I said, "You go tell President Ydigoras that those Cubans should not be used in Puerto Barrios; that if they have landed to keep them at the airport; if they have not landed to return them back to ---" What was the name of that airport?

Anyway the airport nearest the training firica [*sic*]. (Well, apparently the first DC-3, when it came down for landing, was fired upon whereupon the pilot took off immediately, and he was still in the air.)* President Ydigoras sent his own pilot down there to tell these fellows to go back to camp, back to the airport. Before I knew what action had taken place by Ydigoras, the telephone rang, and it was a call from Washington. It was Secretary Christian Herter asking what was underway down there. I told him, and he said, "Well, good. I'm glad you sent word to Ydigoras, but you go over there personally right away and tell him that he's to return those men to the base immediately."

---

* The aircraft were C-46's and, according to a more reliable witness than Muccio, the C-46's were not fired on -- the pilot of the first C-46 mistook guns being fired from escape hatches and ports on his plane for ground fire and didn't stop rolling.

www.ingramcontent.com/pod-product-compliance
Lightning Source LLC
Chambersburg PA
CBHW050458110426
42742CB00018B/3295